"*Susie Hawkins loves the ministry, and her writing reflects her passion. A must read for those who have found themselves in the ever-challenging role of the high call of ministry.*"

DEB GRAHAM
Wife of Pastor Jack Graham,
Prestonwood Baptist Church

"*Finally! A reference manual for ministry wives. This is not just another testimony of what it was like being the wife of a minister, but a tool for those of us who 'have been there and are still doing that' as well as those of you just getting started in this wonderful journey of ministry. Susie has great insight into today's world of ministering to our man, our children, and our church family while keeping a close relationship to the one we are most indebted, Our Lord and Savior. Serving Him alongside our husbands and being happy in the process is possible . . . read more and you'll find out how!*"

JANET A. HUNT
Wife of Pastor Johnny Hunt,
First Baptist Church, Woodstock, Georgia

"*Susie Hawkins' book delivers what it promises. It reads as if one is having an honest conversation with this wise and winsome ministry wife. She is careful not to sugarcoat the disconnects but is also quick to point out the many joys of our high calling. Susie's theological training shines through as she enlightens her readers with interesting anecdotes from church history but especially as she skillfully applies biblical truth. She points us to Scripture at every turn! I highly recommend this much needed and well organized book.*"

MARY K. MOHLER
Wife of President Albert Mohler Jr.,
The Southern Baptist Theological Seminary

"*Susie Hawkins has used her compassionate commitment to woman-to-woman ministries to pen winsome wisdom and mentoring maxims for ministry wives. She works effectively and creatively from her own ministry experiences in a variety of venues to explore the 'connections' available for women who are often isolated and lonely because of the burdens they bear and the tasks they face. Hawkins does not shy away from dealing with the 'disconnects' in life, offering helpful and strategic ways to overcome these challenges and find 'reconnections' in the process. You will laugh and cry, reminisce and meditate, consider options and find answers! This book should not be reserved for women married to ministers. Any woman engaged in serving Christ will find encouragement and inspiration in these readable and edifying pages."*

DOROTHY PATTERSON
Wife of President Paige Patterson,
Southwestern Baptist Theological Seminary
Author, *Where's Mom?* and
coeditor of *Women's Evangelical Commentary*

*"The call to be a ministry wife requires a special blend of gifts, emotions, patience, and leadership. It does not, however, come with a set of instructions or a self-guided 'how to' manual. That is why we must be willing to listen to those voices who can speak knowledge into our lives. Susie Hawkins is one of those voices.*

*In these pages, Susie provides a fresh perspective spoken from experience. And she provides insights and wisdom for your life that will prove to be invaluable as you strive daily to fulfill your God-given, glorious calling as a ministry wife."*

LISA YOUNG
Wife of Pastor Ed Young, Fellowship Church
Author, *The Creative Marriage* and *The Marriage Mirror*

*"Finally, a book full of wise counsel for the ministry wife of the twenty-first century. Through current research, historical and biblical accounts, and heartwarming stories, Hawkins explores the ministry wife's varied connections—with her husband, children, friends, ministry family, herself, and above all, her Lord. She offers sound advice to help ministry wives avoid the pitfalls of criticism, people-pleasing, bitterness, failure and stress. Practical and positive, sometimes challenging conventional wisdom, her book is a goldmine for the ministry wife who desires to honor and complement her husband's work while developing her own unique personhood. I will recommend this book to every ministry wife I encounter."*

DR. SUE EDWARDS
Assistant Professor of Christian Education,
Dallas Theological Seminary
Author, *Leading Women Who Wound:
Strategies for an Effective Ministry*

# from one
# ministry wife
## to another

### honest conversations
### about ministry connections

*Susie Hawkins*

**MOODY PUBLISHERS**
CHICAGO

Editor: Dana Wilkerson
Interior Design: Ragont Design
Cover Design: Barbara Fisher / Levan Fisher Design
Cover Photos: © istockphoto/killerb10 and
          Stockbyte/Getty Imagess/Ryan McVay.

Library of Congress Cataloging-in-Publication Data

Hawkins, Susie.
    From one ministry wife to another : honest conversations about ministry connections / Susie Hawkins.
    p. cm.
    Includes bibliographical references.
    ISBN 978-0-8024-6030-1
    1. Spouses of clergy—Religious life. 2. Women in church work. I. Title.
    BV4395.H324 2009
    253'.22--dc22
                                        2008054597

We hope you enjoy this book from Moody Publishers. Our goal is to provide high quality, thought-provoking books and products that connect truth to your real needs and challenges. For more information on other books and products written and produced from a biblical perspective, go to www.moodypublishers.com or write to:

Moody Publishers
820 N. LaSalle Boulevard
Chicago, IL 60610

1 3 5 7 9 10 8 6 4 2

*Printed in the United States of America*

*To my grandchildren,*
*who have brought me such joy and delight:*
*Halle and Hayes Hermes*
*Jackson, Julia, and Audrey Shivers*

# Contents

Acknowledgments 9

Introduction 11

**Part 1: The Connections**

Chapter 1:   The Historical Connection: Blame It on Katie! 17

Chapter 2:   The Couple Connection: It Takes Two 33

Chapter 3:   The Children Connection: Raising Emotionally
and Spiritually Healthy Children 47

Chapter 4:   The Friendship Connection: Sharing Your Life 69

Chapter 5:   The Church Connection: Relating to the Women
in Your Church 89

Chapter 6:   The Personal Connection: Your Walk with God 109

**Part 2: The Disconnects**

Chapter 7:   The Disconnect of Criticism: Think What They
Would Say if They Really Knew You! 129

Chapter 8:   The Disconnect of Pleasing People: "I'd Be Happy
to Do It!" 143

Chapter 9:   The Disconnect of Bitterness: Pull It Up by the Root 157

Chapter 10: The Disconnect of Failure: Failure Isn't Fatal, but It
Sure Feels That Way 175

Chapter 11: The Disconnect of Stress Fractures: Pressures That
Stress Us 193

**Part 3: The Reconnection**

Chapter 12: The Reconnection: Our Received Ministry 207

Notes 221

# Acknowledgments

There are innumerable people (unfortunately too many to name) over the course of the years who have invested in me and have actually made this volume a reality.

My daughters, Wendy and Holly, as usual, have truly been my greatest encouragers. Their ideas and opinions have been invaluable to me, and I have welcomed their suggestions. Their perspective as "the younger generation" has sharpened me and helped shape my own view of the twenty-first-century ministry wife.

My friends who have prayed for me (you know who you are!) in regard to this project have been a source of enormous support and encouragement as well. Your listening ears, excellent advice, and wise insights have been a source of continual refreshment and strength to me.

I thank Moody Publishers, and especially Jennifer Lyell, for so patiently answering my never-ending questions and for giving me this opportunity.

Finally, thank you to my husband, O. S., who made me a ministry wife! Truly, your belief in me and your persistent encouragement have fueled my desire to complete this project. I love you with all my heart.

# Introduction

*"For most women, the language of conversation is primarily a language of rapport: a way of establishing connections and negotiating relationships."*[1]

—DEBORAH TANNEN

*I* would like to invite you to join me in some honest conversations regarding the life of a ministry wife. This unique culture and calling from God present all of us with challenges and opportunities in this twenty-first century. Today ministry wives live in such diverse settings—some in large cities, others in rural areas. Some are in parachurch ministries, denominational or academic positions, traditional churches, contemporary churches, church plants, or in mission work. Expectations, traditions, and lifestyle differ with each setting. Added to this mix is each woman's individual personality and gifting, as well as her philosophy of ministry. Nevertheless, I believe that ministry wives have much more in common with each other than not. This connection gives us a mutual understanding and appreciation for the sometimes-crazy life we live.

Every woman knows that often the most direct and candid conversations can happen when you least expect them—usually in the kitchen or the ladies' room! As you will see, many of my own conversations with other ministry wives over the years are intertwined with my own story and have become a part of my own philosophy of ministry. I want this book to be a continuation of those conversations, as we explore what it means as wives to be engaged in ministry in our twenty-first-century culture.

I have chosen to use the language of connection, disconnection, and reconnection as the framework of this book. The relationships—or "connections"—we have with our husbands, children, friends, and church families are the heart of our lives and ministry. The "disconnects" are the trials that inevitably come our way and challenge our relationships with others, as well as God. The "reconnection" is the reminder that our ultimate and highest connection is with our Lord Jesus Christ. No matter where our journey takes us, He is already there.

I have experienced church ministry in a small farming community of less than five thousand in population, later moving to town of eleven thousand. A few years later we moved to a sprawling, cosmopolitan city far from the Bible Belt—Fort Lauderdale, Florida. A later move took us to an established, traditional church in downtown Dallas, Texas. As I look back on these experiences, I see where each one brought me a particular perspective and has helped me in determining what I want to say to each of you.

I also am very aware of the thousands of ministry wives who will never write a book or speak publicly on their calling. I want to give them a voice and recognize the valuable and unique ministry they bring to the body of Christ. Only God Himself knows the heartaches and the joys that are part of the fabric of their lives. In one of my illustrations, I mention a small group of ministry wives that I shared with one evening. They were a diverse group as far as ages, types of ministry, interests, and stages of life go. Despite their differences, I marveled as I watched them minister to one another out of the overflow of their own walk with Christ. It is that little group of women I picture in my mind as I write. I can still see the paper plates and cups, the deli potato salad, and the "fixings" left on the table as we sat back and hashed through the challenges that some of them were facing. As I did then, I want this conversation to be practical and realistic, yet within the context of a fervent commitment to Christ and His calling on our lives.

I use the term "ministry wife" as a general expression that is inclusive of the many types of ministries today. The traditional pastor's wife has been joined by the nontraditional ministry wife, and this conversation is for her as well.

Finally, I feel that I owe a debt of gratitude to Oswald and Biddy Chambers. Not until I put my thoughts on paper (or the computer screen), did I realize how *My Utmost for His Highest* has influenced my thinking in spiritual matters throughout my adult life. I include Biddy (Mrs. Oswald Chambers) in this acknowledgment, because if it were not for her, we would not have her husband's works. Her belief in his ministry and her determined efforts to edit and publish his notes after his premature death resulted in a devotional book that is considered a Christian classic. Once again, a ministry wife makes a priceless (and frequently unknown) contribution to the kingdom of God—by supporting the ministry of her husband and using her own gifts and opportunities to share his ministry with the world.

I pray God's blessings on each woman who opens these pages and remind her that "God is not unjust to forget your work and labor of love which you have shown toward His name, in that you have ministered to the saints, and do minister" (Hebrews 6:10).

# PART 1
## The Connections

CONNECTION: a relation of personal intimacy;

a means of communication; a set of persons associ-

ated together; a political, social, professional, or

commercial relationship[1]

# 1

# The Historical Connection:
## *Blame It on Katie!*

"Life is about relationships." If I have heard my husband say that once, I've heard it a million times. Over the course of our lives, this truism has been proven time and time again. We married in 1970, when my husband served as minister to students at the Sagamore Hill Baptist Church in Fort Worth, Texas. (Basically that meant that our dating excursions were primarily to seventh grade boys' go-kart races and middle school retreats.) We then moved on to pastor in Oklahoma and Florida, eventually returning to Texas. Of our years together, twenty-five have been in the pastorate.

Over the years I have noticed something that always occurs when we see someone from one of our former churches. Rarely does anyone ever say to my husband, "I remember your fabulous sermons!" (much to his dismay). And in my case, no one yet has said, "I remember those fabulous dinner parties you gave!" Instead, the conversation always goes like this: "I remember the day you buried my mom," or "I remember when my husband had his heart attack and I looked up in the ER, and there you were," or "I remember when you prayed with me at the altar when my grand-baby was so sick," or "You baptized me and I have never forgotten it," or "You led me to Christ on the beach during spring break." Over and over, we hear (as do many of you) how God used our pitiful attempts at ministry to bring comfort and healing to our congregations. And it is always in the context of a personal connection, the relationship of not only pastor to people, but child of God to child of God.

Our culture cries out for authentic relationships. With the impersonal nature of most communication these days, such as text messaging and e-mailing, the dynamics of genuine relationships are sadly lacking. This is never more important than in the body of Christ, especially in ministry. "It's a bridge called 'relationship' that leads to a land called 'trust.'"[1]

In the context of ministry, it appears to me that a new model for ministry wives has emerged over the last decade. This new model is based on the reality of life as it truly is in the ministry world today. We may not like it or approve of it, but "it is what it is." With the explosion of new church plants filled with people of non-Christian backgrounds and experiences, the traditional expectations of the minister and wife have conformed to the look of our twenty-first century culture. Whether this is good for the cause of Christ or detrimental to it is irrelevant here. My purpose is to identify some of these changes and explore how they currently relate to the life of the ministry wife. Kay Warren has made this observation: "I think pastors' wives today see themselves more as part of an active team. Instead of the husband ahead and the wife behind, I think they see themselves more as side by side."[2]

It is important also to remember that these models are blurry and very general. There are many factors that make up a church's expectations of a minister and his wife, such as local culture, ethnic differences and practices, theological systems, geographical influences, and denominational traditions. Nevertheless, there are some commonalities that can be identified. In order to understand where we have been as ministry wives in the history of the church, it is helpful to see these models from the panorama of a historical perspective.

H. B. London and Neil Wiseman made this observation:

> Through 2,000 years of Christian history, the role of the minister's mate has changed often, and it continues to change rapidly. Even in a single ten- or fifteen-year period, variations have often moved from caring companion to hearth keeper to resident sacrificer to spiritual sustainer to ministry partner to energetic helpmeet to institutional church leader to deputy pastor. But whatever direction the minister's wife's role tilts at any moment of human history, it always involves a position of trusted support for the work of ministry. And it is always an invaluable asset in the service of the kingdom.[3]

## The Ministry Wife in the New Testament

There is not a specific model for ministry wives in the New Testament, despite what many church members may think. No, playing the piano and directing vacation Bible school are not requirements found in the Bible for the preacher's wife. While there are many biblical examples of gifted and wise women, there is no specific description or requirements listed for the wife of a pastor, outside of a few distinguishing, although general, character traits. Some might suggest the stellar New Testament teaching team, Aquila and Priscilla, found in Acts 18. However, while the church met in their home and they actively taught the Word of God together, the Scripture does not specifically identify them in the role of pastor and wife.

In Paul's pastoral epistle to Timothy instructing him on church ministry, he lists the requirements for a pastor (1 Timothy 3:2–7), followed by similar traits to be exhibited in the life of a deacon (vv. 8–10). He then describes the wives of these leaders, listing characteristics which should be found in her: "Likewise, their wives must be reverent, not slanderers, temperate, faithful in all things" (v. 11).

This is the closest thing we have to a list of requirements for the wife of a "bishop" or "overseer." It should be noted that these traits do not reflect giftedness, abilities, or responsibilities, but rather the Christian virtues of reverence, purity of speech, temperance, and faithfulness. Of course these qualities are desired in every Christian woman, not just the wives of ministers.

However, the fact that Paul mentions the Christian character and spiritual maturity of the wife in this passage indicates that her relationship to Christ is significant in how it relates to her husband's calling. This "good work," as Paul describes it in 1 Timothy 3:1, includes the spiritual commitment and character of the wife as she serves Christ and His church alongside her husband. We can conclude that there is not a detailed model for ministry wives in the New Testament, as there is for pastors and elders. The only definitive model is that of a Spirit-filled woman, seeking to follow Jesus with all her heart, developing Christlike characteristics, and walking in wisdom.

## Ministry Wives in the Early Church

The image of the ministry wife in the early church is shadowy, at best. Most of the information on Christian women from this era relates to the martyrs or the desert ascetics, not pastors' wives. However, it would be logical to assume that pastors and their wives ministered together. Tertullian (155–222 CE), an early church theologian and apologist, beautifully described the married couple serving Christ together:

How beautiful, then, the marriage of two Christians, two are one in hope, one in desire, one in the way of life they follow, one in the religion they practice ... both servants of the Master. Nothing divides them, either in flesh or spirit. . . . They pray together, they worship together, they fast together; instructing one another, encouraging one another, strengthening one another. Side by side they visit God's church and partake of God's banquet; side by side they face difficulties and persecution, share their consolations. To such as these [God] gives His peace. Where there are two together, there also He is present.[4]

We can conclude that a husband and wife serving together as partners in the gospel, in spiritual and marital unity, was not unusual in the early church. In fact, Tertullian praises this image and mutual commitment, using it as an example of Christ's presence in the world. The marriage union in a Christian context gave a strong witness for the cause of Christ in the early centuries of the church.

Celibacy for men and women devoted to ministry was practiced in various regions and encouraged by some church leadership with the beginning of the monastic movement around the beginning of the fourth century. Some chose this way of life, believing that celibacy was evidence of one's true separation from the world and physical desires. Others considered celibacy a spiritual gift or practice loosely based on 1 Corinthians 7. (That's one spiritual gift I have never heard anyone request.) While celibacy of the priesthood had been decreed for many years in various regions of the Western church, it wasn't until the twelfth century that ecclesiastical law was ratified, formally requiring celibacy of the clergy.[5] Once the church began to rigidly enforce this doctrine, priests and monks were required to put their wives in convents or leave them. As a result, until the time of the sixteenth century, the small amount of information on women is primarily related to the medieval mystics and other women serving within the boundaries of the established church. But with the onset of the cataclysmic events of the Reformation, the picture of ministry wives began to take shape and become a great deal more interesting.

## The Reformation Model

When Martin Luther nailed his Ninety-five Theses to the door of the Wittenburg Church in Germany, he had no idea that he was starting a monumental religious and cultural shift in Europe that would have aftershocks for years to come. His vehement objections to the corrupt practices of the Roman Catholic Church hit a nerve, and his writings spread like wildfire. One of Luther's many objections to church law and practice was the requirement of celibacy for the priesthood. Soon hundreds, if not thousands, of priests and monks were leaving their posts for areas in Europe that were not under strict Catholic domination. Even nuns in European convents were smuggling in Luther's material and reading it avidly. Earnestly believing in Luther's teachings, one such group, led by Katharina von Bora, escaped the convent at night by way of a cart carrying empty fish barrels.

These women landed literally on the doorstep of the church at Wittenburg, requesting to be married. Luther agreed to this proposal and matched each woman with one of his colleagues, since they also were former priests and monks. Finally, Katharina, who was quite stubborn and picky, proposed that Luther marry her, and after thinking it over, he agreed. The account of their vibrant relationship and deep love and respect for one another is one of the great stories of Christian history. The fascinating aspect of this story is that Katie, as Luther called her, and this motley group of women changed ministry in their culture. They literally and figuratively threw open the door of the parsonage and ministered not only to their husbands and families, but also to church members and the community.

These women did backbreaking labor. They birthed numerous children, tended gardens and livestock, took in widows and orphans, served hundreds of meals a week, ministered to the poor, educated their children, and also took part in lively theological conversations around the dinner table. Katie even brewed her own beer, although I don't recommend anyone trying that today. Having been trained in theology and being quite literate, these women and their offspring brought something to the office of the pastor that the church had not been seen for many years.[6] "Luther's acceptance of children as the core of his rejuvenated life speaks for one of the Reformation's most dramatic shifts. Henceforth the pastor's home, replete with managerial wife and children underfoot, would offer a new model for Protestant couples throughout the world."[7]

Perhaps it is Katie and the other Reformer wives who unintentionally filled in the picture of a ministry wife who not only can somehow manage to do everything on the home front, but is expected to do everything her church desires of her as well. I say, blame it on Katie!

## Traditional/Modern Model

This model is one that has been common to most churches and communities for generations. I suggest that this model is performance-based and is usually what most churches expect and want (or think they want) from their pastor's wife.

This template largely consists of responsibilities or jobs that the church members want to see in the pastors' and staff members' wives, such as musical skills (playing the piano, singing solos), organizational skills (directing vacation Bible school or women's ministry events), or entertaining in the home. While this model works very well for women interested and gifted in these areas, it is difficult for those who are not.

When my husband and I moved to Hobart, Oklahoma, to serve at our first church, I was a bit apprehensive about meeting with the wives of the men on the search committee. However, it was very reassuring for this young, brand-new pastor's wife because they could not have been kinder or more thoughtful and gracious. However, I noticed that the first questions they asked me were, "Do you play the piano?" and "Do you sing?" My answer was "No, I'm so sorry, but I don't!" Some of you readers will identify with me when I tell you that the disappointment on their faces was very obvious. I so wished I could have said yes; however, it would have quickly become clear that while I truly wanted to please them, I had told them a monumental lie.

While most church members say they are happy for the pastor's wife to function as she prefers, the expectations nevertheless have usually been based on her social, public, or organizational skills. It appears that this model is built on the ability of the wife to do the jobs that are expected of her in the church, despite her own gifts or desires. And it should be noted that many of these expectations are unspoken . . . unspoken, that is, until they are not met, in some cases. For an extroverted woman who enjoys people, hospitality, and administrative jobs, this model works well. However, for the more private woman these expectations can be dreadful. These skills may not come naturally to someone like her, and if so, they become a heavy burden to bear. It is the wise woman who works to develop expertise in these areas, yet for some it never comes easily.

On the flip side, the wonderful thing about churches that apply the traditional model is the respect, honor, and care that they usually have for the pastor and his family. One young wife told me that while she was enjoying their new church plant and the nontraditional setting, she missed the genuine care that she and her children received at their former Bible Belt, small town church. There is esteem for the ministry built into this traditional model that is sometimes missing in newer churches. I often told my children that despite some of the annoyances that come with being "PKs" (preacher's kids), they also had the benefit of being prayed for on a daily basis, due to the care and concern of our people. The traditional model has its drawbacks, but also its blessings.

## The Contemporary Model

I do not propose this as a new model, but rather seek to describe what appears to have developed over the last decade in regard to the ministry wife. This pattern is based on the reality of contemporary church culture and is what younger ministry wives who are not in traditional churches are looking to model. New church plants and younger congregations are generally characterized by this generational shift in thinking. A most interesting detailed analysis regarding the distinctiveness of this generation can be found in *The Younger Evangelicals* by Robert E. Webber.[8]

There are three words that seem to best describe newer or less traditional churches and what they are seeking to develop within their faith communities: *authenticity, value,* and *relationships.* Of course, these concepts overlap, but I do believe they best describe the contemporary model of ministry wives that has emerged.

### Authenticity

This is a cliché for this generation—everyone wants "authenticity." What exactly does that mean? Synonyms for this word are *genuineness, legitimacy,* and *validity.* In "Christianese" this translates into "being real." The members of a church want to have a genuine relationship with their ministers and their wives—based on friendship, community, camaraderie, and common goals. While there are varying degrees of an authentic relationship, we can be sure that the expectations of this newer model are based on a ministry wife's transparency, common experiences, and honest conversations—all within the boundaries of what is appropriate, of course.

This authenticity works both ways. It is also what younger ministry wives are seeking for themselves. They may ask, "Can I serve my church in the area where I am truly gifted, not only where

I am expected to serve?" A wife may be expected to teach a women's Bible study or organize church events on a regular basis, especially if the former pastor's wife served in that way (see traditional model). If this is where she is gifted and is something she enjoys, then it works well and everyone is happy. But what if that is not her spiritual gift or skill, much less her real interest? Perhaps her gift is in evangelism or prayer. Will the church give her the freedom to utilize her giftedness in the most effective way? This requires the church members' respect and cooperation as the minister's wife seeks to follow Jesus and use her gifts to strengthen the body of Christ.

> *A*T NO TIME in modern history have ministry wives been as educated or had as many educational opportunities as today.

## Value

This refers to the inherent worth that the wife brings to the ministry partnership of husband and church. It seems that with the onslaught of the Information Age, a yearning to hear and be heard has surfaced. This accounts for the enormous popularity of blogging, which allows anyone with Internet access to voice his or her ideas and opinions in the public arena. Information is couched within one's "story," emphasizing the individual's experience. The phenomenon of YouTube, which allows anyone to demonstrate his or her brilliance or stupidity to the entire world, speaks to this generation's desire to see and be seen. The social interaction and networking that Facebook and MySpace provide online is an indication of the desire to know and be known. Never, in the entire history of the world, has it been possible to connect and interact with as many people as it is now. This is unprecedented and allows a certain customizing of one's social relationships. Those you wish to invite into your space as your "friend" are given access, but those you don't wish to include are denied that access. This is an interesting cultural value and is ultimately reflected in the way the younger generation views ministry wives and vice versa.

A ministry wife's significance, then, is not just related to the fact that she is married to the minister, as some kind of afterthought. Rather, she is perceived as not only his wife, but also a person in her own right, with gifts and skills that enhance not only their ministry together, but also the church as a whole. It should be noted that most evangelical seminaries now recognize this by offering theological education and training for ministry wives, formal and informal. If a woman chooses not to go the traditional theological educational route, there are excellent certificate programs that offer courses in systematic theology, church history, home management, and personal spiritual development for the benefit and enrichment of the wife. At no time in modern history have ministry wives been as educated or had as many educational opportunities as today. This enhances their value to their husbands, as well as to the church body. In the future, this may also lead to wives being employed by the church to serve in their areas of expertise.

## Relationships

There is no question that there is a fascination with relationships in our culture. This is demonstrated every single night on television, with the extreme popularity of reality shows. The combination of seeing people as they really are (authenticity) mixed with the emotion of relationship issues is a recipe for high ratings. While the audience may watch *Survivor* for the gross-out factor (eating live worms, for example), the real questions are, "Who will be voted off the island? And what are the reasons?" This interest in complex and volatile personal relationships in our culture, of course, is carried over into the church.

Those who desire relational authenticity also want personal connections built on transparency, genuine caring, and sharing. In the traditional model previously mentioned, the ministry wife is "put on a pedestal" by the congregation to be admired and imitated in what she does and how she does it. She represents to some the model of perfection. I seriously doubt if many younger ministry wives (and probably a great number of older ones also) want to be on a pedestal, since it looks really lonely up there.

Shaping this newer model is the need Christian women have for a standard in developing authentic Christlike characteristics as wives, moms, friends, and leaders, according to Titus 2:1–5. For the women who were not raised in Christian homes or churches, this modeling is crucial to their own spiritual growth and understanding. No one needs to know how to act like a Christian at church; it's the day-to-day responsibilities, schedules, and conflicts that call for genuine faith and obedience. One thing women my age hear over and over is the desire of younger women to be shown what it looks like to live as a Christian wife and mom. They desperately need to be mentored and befriended by older Christian women who can demonstrate how to navigate the challenges that come with following Christ in a twenty-first century world. It is no coincidence that many of our newer churches, pastored by younger men, have developed mission statements that emphasize discipleship and faith, within the context of a community made up of authentic relationships.

It is these three words, then, that I believe best describe the contemporary model for the ministry wife. *Authentic* people *valuing* one another for who they are, loving and living in the context of *relationships* is the primary need of the younger generation today.

## An Illustration of the Contemporary Model

A clear illustration of this newer model can be seen today in the political realm. It is obvious that there are parallels in the lives of ministry wives and political wives. While there is no specific requirement (legal or otherwise) for a woman to function in either capacity, there is a heavy load of expectations as well as opportunities that come with both positions. The wife of a minister, just like the wife of a politician, can greatly enhance her husband's career, or she can be a detriment to it. While I personally do not believe that, generally speaking, a wife can "make or break" her husband (except in extreme situations), her influence on her husband is undoubtedly very effective. Never underestimate the power of pillow talk!

However, in our contemporary culture, this spousal influence seems to have taken a more visible and intentional turn. As I write this, we are just coming out of a presidential election season, and a new political power couple with enormous appeal has burst on the scene: Barack and Michelle Obama. Let me be clear that this is in no way an endorsement of their political views. However, I do believe that Michelle Obama illustrates this contemporary model. It is intriguing to watch her as she speaks and interacts with her husband on the national stage. I believe she personifies this newer model, although she is in the political—not ministerial—world.

First, Michelle is authentic—she says exactly what she thinks. This trait may give her husband and his advisors headaches in the future, but she appears to be a contemporary woman who speaks her mind. Of course, that may not always be wise since there is great wisdom in discernment and self-control. Obviously it is best to find ways to phrase harsh thoughts or negative emotions that are not offensive or inappropriate. However, our culture values (or claims to) transparency and honesty, not just political rhetoric. Michelle, who is a gifted communicator, comes across as authentic and quite confident in her husband's and political party's ability to reach their goals.

Second, Michelle brings political weight and value to her husband's campaign. Her law degree from Harvard and her experience in the workforce complement her husband's political ambitions and policies. Her knowledge of law and the political system clearly enhance her husband's image and style, as does her public speaking ability. However, education is only one way value is measured. Any talent, interest, or expertise can be useful or helpful, particularly in ministry, if it encourages relationships, strengthens believers, and provides opportunities for teaching as well as enjoyment.

Finally, Michelle seems to relish the relationship she has with her husband and daughters. Along with her skill in politics, she is a devout mother, often mentioning her daughters in her speeches. It is quite clear that she is a strong advocate for her children and is very competent in managing the family household. In other words, it appears that Michelle hasn't minimized familial bonds or sacrificed commitment to her children and husband for the political arena, as some have done in the past. Even in their interaction on stage, this new model is evident. During onstage introductions, husbands and wives normally give the obligatory affectionate hug and pat on the back." The Obamas, however, add another component to this visual—the "fist bump." This newer gesture indicates a vibrant partnership and teamwork, and it says, "We are in this together, baby!" All three of these components are evident in Michelle, and it will be interesting to observe the development of this image in political wives in the future.

## Application for Today

WHAT DOES ALL of this mean to us as ministry wives? It means that if we wish to have a voice and an influence in the body of Christ relating to our current culture, we must strive for authenticity, yet always be aware of the appropriate boundaries.

We are reminded that we are valued not only for our contributions to our families, churches, and ministries, but also to the body of Christ as a whole and to the work of the kingdom. And finally, we must always remember that "life is about relationships"—with our Lord Jesus Christ, our spiritual family, our earthly families, and even ourselves.

*Reflection*

---

THE THREE WORDS pinpointed in this chapter are good to examine in light of our own lives and ministry.

◆ Am I authentic? Do I feel free to be who I am? Am I willing to let others be authentic also?

◆ How do I bring value to the ministry? What are my gifts and interests? What do I take pleasure in sharing with others?

◆ Can I remember that connecting with people and living in true community with them is more important than any responsibility in the church? What might I need to change in my life to reflect this belief?

# 2

# The Couple Connection:
## *It Takes Two*

"*W*ill you take this man—for better, for worse, for richer, for poorer, in sickness and in health, to love and to cherish, until death do you part?"[1]

Most of us hear these words in some variation at our wedding altars. Starry-eyed and in love, we cannot imagine not living together as a couple in blissful harmony forever. However, as we all know, it doesn't take long for reality to set in. The title of one of Florence Littauer's books, *After Every Wedding Comes a Marriage,* expresses this truth quite succinctly. However, marriage issues are often even more pressing when the couple is in ministry. Many excellent books have been written to expressly address the unique needs of the ministry marriage. My major intent, however, is to explore the couple's call to ministry and to see what it looks like in the twenty-first century.

## The Call to Ministry:
## "Whom shall I send?" (Isaiah 6:8)

"Calling" in the New Testament usually refers to the Holy Spirit's inward call to the individual for conversion. As believers, the Spirit called each of us at some point to yield our lives to Jesus. However, there is another type of calling, and that is the calling to a career or vocational ministry. This call can be mysterious, bewildering, and wonderful, all at the same time. The general understanding of being called into ministry is that God calls a person to this task—we do not call ourselves or just decide to go into this profession.

The Scripture gives us numerous illustrations of men and women that God called to carry out His work. In the Old Testament we have the stories of Abraham, Moses, Joshua, Deborah, Samuel, David, Esther, and the prophets—all who were called to lead the children of Israel. The New Testament is full of examples of those whom God called—different circumstances, but the same principle. Mary, Elizabeth, Matthew, John, James, Andrew, Peter and the rest of the disciples, Paul, and others experienced an unexpected call by Jesus on their lives. The Old Testament prophet Isaiah described the call in this way, "I heard the voice of the Lord, saying: 'Whom shall I send, and who will go for Us?' Then I said, 'Here am I, send me!'" (Isaiah 6:8). God has chosen to call ministers to lead His church and then equip them for this task. Moses' call was more direct: "Come now, therefore, and I will send you to Pharaoh that you may bring My people, the children of Israel, out of Egypt" (Exodus 3:10).

God's call on the life of a ministry wife may be general or very direct; there is no particular mode. Some have had a personal calling into service, as they sought God's will for their lives—perhaps in a collegiate or single-adult setting, or even at a younger age. Whether they married or not, they were committed to this task and actively sought to prepare themselves or find opportunities for ministry. Others sense a call later, perhaps when their husbands feel led by the Spirit to make a move into a ministerial position or job. There is really no biblical prototype for specifically how a call to ministry comes; the important thing is recognizing and obeying it. Oswald Chambers says:

> The realization of the call in a person's life may come like a clap of thunder or it may dawn gradually. But however quickly or slowly this awareness comes, it is always accompanied with an undercurrent of the supernatural. . . . Paul describes is as a compulsion that was placed upon him.[2]

The more crucial issue is this: understanding and embracing the truth that if your husband is called to ministry, then you are called also, because *you are one.* The basis for this is found in Genesis 2, which gives us the biblical narrative regarding the foundation and concept of marriage:

> And the Lord God said, "It is not good that man should be alone; I will make a helper comparable to him. . . . And the Lord God caused a deep sleep to fall on Adam, and he slept; and He took one of his ribs, and closed up the flesh in its place. Then the rib which the Lord God had taken from man He made into a woman, and He brought her to the man. And Adam said: "This is now bone of my bones and flesh of my flesh; she shall be called Woman, because she was taken out of Man." Therefore a man shall leave his father and mother and be joined to his wife, and they shall become one flesh. And they were both naked, the man and his wife, and were not ashamed (Genesis 2:18, 21–25).

There are several points in this text that speak to the spiritual unity—or oneness—of marriage. The passage begins with God's declaration that "it is not good that man should be alone." (Were truer words ever spoken?) There is something in a man that is incomplete, generally speaking, when he is without a wife. The Hebrew literally says, "The being of man by himself is no good."

I have marveled at this truth over the years we have spent in church work. How many times have we seen a brokenhearted man who has been widowed quickly remarry? Sometimes that is a good thing, and sometimes it is not so good—and it can be challenging for the children involved. But it continually demonstrates this basic truth of life: a man needs a woman to help him. Women are gifted by God with life managerial skills and are adept at creating a fulfilling and meaningful life, whether married or not. While I may be generalizing, the point is that a man needs a wife, and never more than when he is in ministry. Life experience proves this point.

Second, God stated that He would make Adam "a helper comparable to him."

In English, the word *helper* usually denotes an assistant or someone in a subordinate role. However, in the Hebrew, this word carries a different nuance. A helper (*ezer*) does for someone what he cannot do for himself. The note in the New English Translation Bible says, "In this context the word seems to express the idea of an 'indispensable companion.'"[3]

*E*VE WAS CREATED to stand beside Adam— not as an inferior partner—but as an equal person, with a unique function—helper.

This word is used in a similar way in Psalm 54:4, where David says, "Behold, God is my helper." David's prayer in this psalm is for God to deliver him from his adversaries. He begs God to save him, vindicate him, and hear his prayer. When he speaks of God as his helper, he is speaking of his desperate need for assistance—he cannot do this alone. This usage indicates the fuller meaning of *helper.* (Also see Psalm 33:20; 46:1; 94:17; 115:9; 118:13; 1 Samuel 7:12; Isaiah 49:8.)

God then describes this helper as "comparable to him." Other versions use "suitable" (NIV, NASB) or "corresponds" (NET) in translating this term. The Hebrew literally says, "according to the opposite of him." Again, the NET Bible has an excellent note: "The man's form and nature are matched by the woman's as she reflects him and complements him. Together they correspond. In short, this prepositional phrase indicates that she has everything that God had invested in him."[4] Eve was created to stand beside Adam— not as an inferior partner—but as an equal person, with a unique function—helper.

In the text (Genesis 2:22–24), God marries Adam and Eve, and they "become one flesh"—one flesh physically, emotionally, and spiritually (v. 24). The narrator's quotation of Adam's words emphasizes their importance in the account, "This one, at last, is bone of my bone, and flesh of my flesh, this one will be called woman for she was taken out of man" (v. 23 NET). The narrator then explains, "That is why a man leaves his father and mother and unites with his wife, and they become a new family."

This word *unites* is often translated as "cleaves to" and is the same word used in Ruth 1:14, when Ruth refused to leave Naomi. This describes a relationship of two individuals who have been blended into one unit in relationship, reflecting a change of condition.

The united couple becomes "one flesh" (NKJV)—"a new family" (NET). This refers to more than a physical or sexual union. The two become legally related, with a oneness in all aspects of life, building a future together.

What does all of this mean to ministry wives in particular? If our husbands are called to ministry, then we share that calling also. This negates any wife saying, "My husband is called, but I certainly am not." You may not be employed by a church as he is, but that does not mean you do not share a calling by God to ministry.

A ministry wife is called—as a partner—to serve alongside her husband. She should feel free, as opportunities and the seasons of life unfold, to use her gifts and abilities according to this holy calling. In doing so, she fulfills God's purpose in her life as wife and ministry companion.

Barbara Hughes puts it this way:

> The Incarnate Son of God beautifully demonstrated that all of us are to be servants (John 13). Later, when he was comforting his disciples with the promise of the Holy Spirit, he referred to him as "another Helper" (John 14:16). By addressing him (the Third Person of the Godhead) as a helper, he forever elevated the position of the one who assists. As we trace the Holy Spirit's actions through the New Testament, we find him repeatedly encouraging, comforting, coming alongside, and helping. The work of the Holy Spirit, the helper is beautiful! And women are never more lovely than when they follow his example, cherishing their function as helper. There is no better word to describe the role of a pastor's wife than this—helper. It is not demeaning and we must not despise it. It is divine.[5]

Again, this truth does not translate into having to work for the church or taking on responsibilities no one else in the church wants. It doesn't mean she has to play the piano or organ, sing solos, direct vacation Bible school, or bake cookies for the nursing home. It does mean that she should discover and use her spiritual gifts (with the encouragement and support of her husband) and find opportunities to utilize and enjoy them among the community and church.

## The Unwanted Call: "Lord, Please! Send Anyone Else." (Exodus 4:13 NLT)

All of the above sounds great theoretically. However, it would be less than authentic to presume that every ministry wife has welcomed and embraced this call. It is not all that unusual to hear a wife privately say that she never wanted to be in ministry and struggles daily with its demands. Most of these women genuinely love their husbands and are genuine Christians. What is there to say to women in these situations?

In R.T. Kendall's book *The Thorn in the Flesh,* he explores the theme of the believer's continuing struggle with a particular trial. Based on Paul's admission in 2 Corinthians 12:7, Kendall suggests that Paul's "thorn" is a situation in one's life that probably will never disappear. ("And lest I should be exalted above measure by the abundance of the revelations, a thorn in the flesh was given to me, a messenger of Satan to buffet me, lest I be exalted above measure.") This thorn is a metaphor for a constant problem or pain that hurts, hinders, and vexes us. It could be one's marital state, a physical problem, an emotional problem, or a myriad of other circumstances we struggle with in this fallen world. Paul states that the purpose of his thorn was to keep him humble, and we may be assured that God's purposes for our thorns are the same.

One of these thorns may be an unwanted call to ministry, according to Kendall. He describes it this way:

> It is having to spend your life doing what by choice you wouldn't have preferred at all—but your talent is best suited for something else. As for your education, it all seems to have gone down the drain. You went to university to study this, and now look at what you are having to do for a living! When it comes to where God has put you, you may feel over-qualified and frustrated. Or you may feel under-qualified and frustrated. It may also be that you are required to work with people you would never have chosen to work with. It may also be that you are in a place you would never have chosen to be. You are having to live and work in a place which is the last place on earth you wanted to be.[6]

There are numerous biblical examples of our spiritual heroes who faced an unwelcome call. Moses did not want to go to Pharaoh and argued vehemently with God over it. Joseph certainly did not feel called to Egypt, nor did he deserve to go to prison, but Scripture shows us that it was the providence of God in his life. Abraham, Daniel and his friends in exile, Nehemiah, Esther, Jonah, Paul, Simon Peter, and many others struggled with an unwanted call. And yet, with the advantage of hindsight and biblical revelation, we can clearly see God's purposes accomplished through their lives. For some reason known only to God, He has chosen to do His work through His servants, as weak and unwilling as they sometimes are.

Kendall comes to this conclusion: "The way we have been led we cannot understand at the time, but time shows there is purpose and meaning in it all. So with you. God knows your potential, and it may seem wasted at first, but one day you will see a reason."[7]

If you feel that you are living with an unwanted call on your life, then that is something that must be seriously addressed with prayer and solid biblical counsel. One thing is for certain: you are not alone in feeling that way. It is difficult to let go of our personal dreams and aspirations, but there are times we must face reality and deal with life on its own terms. The good news is that we, like those who have gone before us, find the grace that Paul talks about in this passage (2 Corinthians 12:9). God's grace was sufficient for Paul, and it will be sufficient for you and the call to ministry.

## Serving as Partners: "Having Concluded That God Was Calling Us . . ." (Acts 16:10 NLT)

What does this marriage connection look like in the context of partnering together in ministry? Examples from history paint a vibrant and diverse picture of husbands and wives answering God's call on their lives.

Priscilla and Aquila, Paul's co-laborers, are a biblical illustration of a couple serving together in ministry (Acts 18:1–3, 26; Romans

16:3; 1 Corinthians 16:19; 2 Timothy 4:19). Although we have limited information about them, we can draw some conclusions about their ministry together. Having fled Italy due to persecution, they were living in Corinth, where they met up with Paul. Sharing his occupation as tent makers, they worked and evangelized with him. After approximately eighteen months, they accompanied Paul and sailed to Syria, stopping in Ephesus.

Scripture records that there they had an encounter with the newly converted Apollos, who was a skilled orator, yet lacked some doctrinal knowledge. They privately "took him aside and explained to him the way of God more accurately" (Acts 18:26). Paul mentions his appreciation for them more than once in his epistles and also acknowledges that they "risked their own necks" for him in Romans 16:4, indicating their return to their homeland and the establishment of a church there. Interestingly enough, Priscilla could have been one of the first bi-vocational pastor's wives in the early church.

While this is all the information we have on this couple, we know enough to observe that they were coworkers in the gospel with each other, with Paul, and with other believers. While we do not know exactly what Paul meant when he said they risked their lives for him, we can be sure that their lives were in danger in some way, whether from persecution by the Jews or the Romans. This is significant—they were courageous and passionate believers. We can also conclude that Priscilla's hospitable home was open for church worship services and meetings, as well as providing hospitality for other believers, such as Paul. She clearly took an active role in teaching and discipling in the first century church, and she was skilled in a profession (tent-making) as well (Acts 18:3).

As previously mentioned, throughout church history there is a pattern of ministry wives serving faithfully and effectively alongside their husbands, following in the footsteps of Priscilla. Some of these women took very public roles, yet others served and supported the ministry God gave them in a quieter and less visible role. The common factor in these cases seems to be the wife finding her niche, recognizing her own gifts and interests, and following God's call in obedience alongside her husband.

Catherine Booth (1829–1890) was a woman whose shared ministry was quite public. As the founders of The Salvation Army, Catherine and her husband, William, worked tirelessly with the poor in London's East End. Reacting to the local churches' lack of concern for the plight of the poor, the Booths began a ministry of social action, evangelism, and discipleship. Their shared vision, coupled with their leadership skills, resulted in hundreds of volunteers working diligently with alcoholics, prostitutes, and other troubled souls in the ghettos of London during the nineteenth century. Due to her skills and foresight, Catherine's role soon grew from administrative responsibilities and counseling new Christians to public evangelism in their tent meetings. Her zeal for the gospel and for the salvation of souls was the heart of their ministry. This organization exists today as one of the world's foremost ministries to the poor. Two of the Booths' eight children were responsible for bringing the work of The Salvation Army to America, and several of their descendants have stayed active in the organization. Catherine relished her visible and active role and used every opportunity and drop of physical energy she had to further the gospel.

On the other end of the spectrum stands her contemporary, Susannah Spurgeon (1832–1892), wife of renowned pastor Charles Haddon Spurgeon of the Metropolitan Tabernacle, also in London. Susannah was not a public speaker or teacher like Catherine Booth was. Her contribution was primarily through the establishment of the Book Fund, which was begun in order to provide Spurgeon's books and commentaries as resources for rural pastors who could not afford to purchase them.

After proofreading one of her husband's books, Susannah remarked that she wished she could put a copy of the book in the hands of every minister in England.[8] Spurgeon challenged her to do so, and after examining her own small savings from her household funds, she found that she would be able to purchase one hundred copies to give away. This was the first step in her establishment of the Book Fund. Once the Book Fund was announced in Spurgeon's paper, *The Sword and the Trowel,* over two hundred ministers applied for the book. Much to her relief, she was able to supply each applicant. Soon other donors began to support the Book Fund, which continued to supply needy ministers with preaching resources for many years. She continued her interest in literary matters, eventually penning an autobiography of her husband entitled, *C. H. Spurgeon's Autobiography, Compiled from His Letters, Notes, and Diaries.* Susannah also wrote a volume on the development of the Book Fund as well as several devotional books.

Due to the difficult birth of their twin boys, Susannah suffered physically the rest of her life and was often bedridden. Nevertheless, her partnership with her husband in his pastoral ministry was remarkable, despite her health problems. She knew all too well the struggles and difficulties these penniless pastors and their families endured, and she creatively used her gifts and ingenuity to find a way to meet those needs. Although she was not as visible and physically active as Catherine Booth, she too made a distinct contribution to the work of the kingdom. I admire her enormously—for her creativity, resourcefulness, and perseverance in finding her place in ministry, and for using her gifts and interests to further the work of the gospel in England. The ministries of both of these women greatly complemented their husbands' ministries and increased their influence then as well as in the future.

My heart goes out to men who are struggling to pastor or minister without the emotional or spiritual support of their wives. In light of the heavy responsibilities that are put on anyone in ministry, it is essential that a husband be encouraged by his wife—this is a vital part of serving as partners. Occasionally I have heard someone say, "He may be called, but I am not." If you find yourself in this camp, I urge you to reconsider this line of thinking and to begin to ask God to give you the grace and the desire to be willing to serve alongside your husband, sharing his call. Of course, this might lead to a woman saying that she is not confident her husband was ever called to ministry at all, much less that she was called. If that is the case, then some solid marriage and spiritual counseling is in order as soon as possible. Even if you do not choose to take on responsibilities in your particular ministry, your prayer and emotional support is vital to the couple connection. Oswald Chambers ends his devotional, *The Awareness of the Call* with these wise words, "If you will agree with God's purpose, He will bring not only your conscious level but also all the deeper levels of your life, which you yourself cannot reach, into perfect harmony."[9]

Esther Burroughs, a ministry wife, author, and speaker whom I greatly respect, relates this story of her father and mother, who pastored various small churches in the Midwest. I have never forgotten it because it so poignantly illustrates the true *agape* love of a wife who humbly and quietly sought to honor God by simply serving alongside her husband. While this speaks to a previous generation, to me the spirit of this woman is like a sweet fragrance, carried over the years, that touches us and exhorts us today.

One day while visiting with my mom before she passed away in 1996, she asked me if I ever spoke to ministers' wives. I replied that yes, I did. My mother then told me that she had shared with a group of young ministers' wives recently and told them that every Sunday morning she would lay out her husband's clothes on the bed for him—his suit, tie, hanky, socks, and shoes. She was surprised when they all laughed, because she had not meant it to be humorous. Their response was, "Let them dress themselves!"

I remembered my mom doing this very thing, and so I asked her why she did it. Quietly my mother responded, "I did it so that your father could have more time in prayer before God as he prepared to open the Word of God for the people of God." I was pierced by my mother's words and was convicted that I had not made a similar effort to serve my minister husband, especially on Sunday mornings.

The next Sunday, while my husband, Bob, was eating breakfast, I slipped into the bedroom and laid out his clothes, just as I had seen my mother do for my father so many times. When he came into the bedroom, he saw his clothes on the bed and asked what in the world I was doing. I told him that I was laying out his clothes for him. He said, "Thanks, but I've been dressing myself on Sundays for all these years, and I don't really need any assistance."

I replied, "I was just trying to help, and besides, I think you are supposed to be praying!" We laughed together as I shared the conversation I had just had with my mother.

Esther sees her mother's efforts as an act of worship to God and quiet service to their people. She poses the question, "What might happen in the homes of the ministers all across the world if wives did something on Sabbath morning to make it possible for their minister-husbands to have more time on their knees before God as they prepared to speak the Word of God to the people of God?"

She then suggested how our families might be affected if on Monday morning, the father would get the lunches ready and help with breakfast, so the mother could be on her knees in prayer for her children as they go off to school that day and for her husband as he goes to the workplace. She believes we would see a difference in our children, husbands, and communities. Who could disagree?

In their book *Married to a Pastor's Wife*, H. B. London and Neil Wiseman put it wisely, "Regardless, then, of the pastor's wife's style of establishing and maintaining association with the church, she must bring a spiritually sensitive, quality person to the relationship. . . . The task of shared ministry is a trust from God more than a demand from any congregation."[10]

*Reflection*

---

◆ Can you identify how or when you felt called to ministry? My own experience was not in line with the "normal" call, but more like a gradual dawning, as Oswald Chambers put it.[11] While I loved the Lord and desired to follow Him in my life, I never really thought about ministry until I fell in love with my husband and knew we would marry. In light of that, I assumed I was called to ministry as well. Remembering the circumstances of your call and the spiritual markers that usually accompany it will help you remember what you do and why you do it.

◆ How do you see your gifts and interests fitting in with your husband's? Usually in God's economy, the strengths and weaknesses of the husband and wife team balance out very well.

◆ Kent and Barbara Hughes faced a crisis in ministry and wrote an excellent book out of that experience called *Liberating Ministry from the Success Syndrome.* Barbara makes some very practical and biblically based points in her chapter on how a pastor's wife can truly help her husband. However, nothing is more important than earnestly praying for your husband faithfully, bringing every detail of his life before God.[12]

# 3

# The Children Connection:
## *Raising Emotionally and Spiritually Healthy Children*

*D*enzel Washington, Marvin Gaye, Condoleezza Rice, Alice Cooper (yes, *that* Alice Cooper), and Jessica Simpson—what do these random people have in common? You probably guessed it. They are all preachers' kids, also known as "PKs." Any serious discussion of ministry life must include a close look at the life of ministry children. Often thrust into the limelight, and often given unreasonable expectations, PKs sometimes struggle with unique challenges only experienced by other PKs. Generally speaking, there are two stereotypical views of ministry kids: that they are rebellious little hellions who make life miserable for their parents and their church, or that they are obnoxious, self-righteous kids who thoroughly enjoy preaching sin and destruction to their peers.

Of course, neither extreme is usually true. Most PKs manage to find their way and end up as emotionally and spiritually healthy adults. However, it does require discernment, skill, and insight to parent PKs and help them navigate the sometimes rough waters of being a child of a minister.

We can learn at least one very general but helpful lesson from our predecessors. Ministry couples of past generations did not have the advantage of all the parenting resources we have these days, nor did they have many opportunities to have transparent and candid discussions with anyone (especially in their churches) regarding their children. It just wasn't done. In fact, I would say it is only in the last thirty years that these topics have been introduced in the public forum and openly written about and discussed. I would suggest, as have many others, that unintentionally many pastors have sacrificed their family time in order to serve the church. In short, church came first. Let me be clear that I do *not* think that this was ever intentional in the life of any family. Ministry parents love their children just as much as anyone else and know that their children need their parents' emotional investment as much as any others do. However, as we all know, unless a parent vigilantly watches the church calendar and family schedules, potential time spent together as a family vanishes into thin air. When time together is lost, the opportunities to teach, share, and just enjoy one another's company is lost as well.

In 1993 we moved to Dallas, Texas, when my husband, O. S., became pastor of First Baptist Church, succeeding the legendary W. A. Criswell. The Criswells were a wonderful couple, and we were greatly blessed to have their support and friendship. O. S. loved Dr. C (as he was called) dearly, counting him as a father in the ministry. In Dr. Criswell's declining years, O. S. would frequently go to his home to visit with him. On one of those occasions, O. S. asked him, "Preacher, if you had it to do all over again, is there anything you would do differently?" Without a second's hesitation, and with tears quickly filling his eyes, Dr. Criswell answered, "Yes, son, there is. I would have devoted more time to my family. My priorities were

God, then the church, and then my family."

I appreciate Dr. Criswell's honesty and his admission that his family did not receive the attention that it should have. Perhaps this accounts to some degree for the years of painful estrangement between the Criswells and their daughter. Thankfully, a very sweet reconciliation was made before his death, and they had some years to truly enjoy each other's company. Nevertheless, many pastors of his generation unintentionally fell into the same pattern of thinking, and they inevitably had poor relationships with their adult children.

There is a tension that will always exist between time spent working in ministry and time spent with the family. Many resources exist to help parents find this balance and maintain a strong family life in the home. I do believe, however, that ministry parents have an added burden in this arena, due to the extraordinary time pressures put on a church pastor or staff member. There is no end to the needs that must be met, and it is inevitable that there will be constant challenges in this area. It takes deliberate planning and a watchful eye on the calendar to maintain the balance needed in the ministry home. To guard family time, we must be able to discern the "good" from the "best."

It is the spiritual responsibility of parents to train and teach their children. Despite all the time pressures that come with ministry life, we cannot fail to fulfill the commands given in Scripture to make the time to personally nurture our children in the ways of the Lord. And it should go without saying that no matter how much slack Mom may pick up for Dad, it never excuses or even remotely makes up for a lack of paternal nurturing and teaching. Dorothy Patterson makes a good point on this topic—that as ministers fulfill their responsibilities to their own children, they will be modeling that very thing for their people.

The Lord shows in another way how seriously He holds ministry fathers accountable to their family responsibilities. A minister who does not accept his duties to wife and children does not meet the biblical qualifications for kingdom ministries. A pastor must manage his own family well . . . and see that his children obey him with proper respect (see 1 Timothy 3:1–7). A minister father must provide spiritual training for his children, investing whatever time is necessary to disciple his children. He not only provides what is needed for the spiritual nurturing of his children but also models for his congregation an important responsibility given by the Lord to husbands and fathers.[1]

## God Has No Grandchildren

The most important area of all in raising PKs, as any other children, is giving vigilant attention to their spiritual lives. Ironically, even in ministry, without realizing it, parents can default to assuming others are teaching spiritual values to their children, such as Bible study leaders or Sunday school teachers.

A number of years ago I read an interesting book entitled *The Dangers of Growing Up in a Christian Home* by Donald Sloat.[2] This book was highly influential in my approach to parenting my PKs at that time. Those of you who were raised in an evangelical home will immediately identify with Sloat's illustrations and thoughtful points. (I guarantee they will bring a smile to your face.) He depicts some of the unintended barriers that often hinder a child's spiritual growth and understanding, such as parental hypocrisy, neglect of children's feelings and opinions, use of guilt to manipulate, legalism, and others.

Sloat is very appreciative of the heritage he received from his parents, and the book is in no way an exposé. Instead, it's an honest evaluation of his upbringing, along with excellent suggestions about how not to unintentionally fall into poor parenting habits, especially as they relate to spiritual values in the Christian home. Building our children's spiritual heritage is first and foremost our responsibility, not someone else's. Praying for them, talking through their doubts and questions, explaining the "whys" of our own church traditions and practices, and helping them as they grow in Christ are all parts of the exhortation to "bring [your children] up in the training and admonition of the Lord" (Ephesians 6:4). As the old saying goes, "God has no grandchildren." The children of every generation must seek their own relationship with Him. While we cannot pass on our salvation to our children, we certainly can train them for spiritual service and prepare them for the time when they will begin their own walk with Christ. This is especially true in the lives of PKs.

## Teach Your PKs Well

During our child-raising years, certain sayings or phrases would catch our attention and quickly become part of our parenting philosophy. Without realizing it, we eventually noticed that each saying reflected a valuable principle for both parent and child. We also found that as our children grew and moved through the different stages of life, each of these sayings continued to remind us of certain truths and kept us focused on principles, not just rules. Biblical principles differ from rules in that principles can be applied at any age or any setting. Rules relate more to specific times, places, and actions. Generally speaking, household rules are born out of principles that Mom and Dad value and seek to follow. Each of the following sayings also relate well to the PKs' world and their unique place in our culture.

### Kids Are People, Too! (Respect)

When our daughter Wendy was around five years old, I bought her a T-shirt that said, "Kids are people, too!" This little phrase was quickly incorporated into our family conversations (especially when she and her sister were protesting something). Even though it was just a cute saying on a cute T-shirt, this little phrase served as a reminder to us that all healthy relationships must contain the cornerstone of respect, especially the parent-child connection.

Respecting your children simply means that you give them the space and the right to be an individual in the family structure. You listen to them, help them develop their gifts and skills according to their own interests, and relate to them according to their personality type.

Kids are just little people growing into big people. They are born with their own personalities, gifts, desires, and interests. Of course a child's environment enormously influences him or her (that's another discussion), but all parents have undoubtedly marveled at how some things are just "in" a child. Every child is "fearfully and wonderfully made" (Psalm 139:14). Their future personalities and interests are in their DNA, and each little child is a potential adult—a person. Respecting who God made them to be as people is fundamental in developing a healthy relationship with your children.

*THE WISE PARENT takes the child's personality into consideration when making decisions regarding that particular child's education, discipline, and interests.*

Nothing has helped me more in managing relationships and understanding people (especially our children) than the study of the temperaments. I was first introduced to them through the books of Dr. Tim LaHaye and Florence Littauer.[3] Their premise was that each person is born with a "temperament," or personality type. While there are four basic temperaments, everyone is a blend of two or maybe three of them. This means that every individual is unique and sees the world according to his or her own perspective. Understanding your child's temperament is invaluable in helping you understand his or her "operating system." The wise parent takes the child's personality into consideration when making decisions regarding that particular child's education, discipline, and interests. It communicates respect for the person God made him or her to be.

Every family has an amazing balance of the personality types. I remember sitting with our teenage girls at the kitchen table one time, telling them a heartbreaking story about a woman in our church. Our sensitive daughter, Holly, sat listening to me with tears welling up in her brown eyes. Her first reaction was, "How awful for her! Is there anything we can do to help her?" Our older daughter, Wendy (of the choleric temperament), sat listening to me with no facial expression at all, her arms crossed. Her only comment: "I don't feel sorry for her. It's her own fault." It's probably no surprise that Wendy became an attorney and Holly earned a master's degree in counseling.

Another aspect of respect is acknowledging a child's destiny. Giving your children a mind-set toward their futures is important. Discussing important questions of the future even when they are young motivates them to think: What will I be? What do I want to do? What can I do well? Where do I want to live? What does God have for me to do on this earth? What can I contribute? Asking these questions helps your children formulate their dreams and provides a sense of security regarding God's providence and His will for their lives.

When our girls were in their teen years, we had a bulletin board near the kitchen phone with the family calendar on it along with the usual assortment of notes and business cards. As they grew interested in the opposite sex, I began putting a few pictures of boys on the bulletin board that I thought were good models for future husbands. Some of them they had met on our family trips, some were the sons of my friends, and some they barely knew. Of course I did not actually intend or even particularly want for either girl to marry a particular person; I simply was attempting to communicate that thinking and praying now about the type of person you will marry is a really good thing to do. To win a spot on the bulletin board meant that a young man had good manners, had an idea of what he wanted to do in life, respected others, and had a strong Christian commitment. The point of the bulletin board was to give our girls a visual reminder that choosing a marriage partner was so important that it deserved their time and attention long before it actually happened. It did not surprise me when Wendy called us and told us about a young man named Brian she had met in law school and with whom she was very impressed. Her comment was, "Mom, he's one for the bulletin board." He became our son-in-law.

Tracy Osborne, a PK herself, has collected data on the lives of ministry children over the past decade for her master's thesis.[4] She identifies ten major stressors in their lives: unrealistic expectations, lack of privacy, time constraints, financial stain, frequent moves, isolation, image preservation, congregational interference in parenting, emotional needs being ignored, and the difficulty in keeping information secret. Each one of these deserves its own chapter, but I will leave that for Tracy to address! At any rate, it is good to look closely at each of these stressors and determine if it relates to your children, and if so, how best to handle it.

In my opinion, respect takes on an added dimension in the PK world. Ministry parents may need to be a little more protective regarding their children's privacy. While ministers and wives who are public speakers usually feel free to share family illustrations, it is good to remember that you may have a child who doesn't appreciate something about them being told to the whole church.[5] It is a parent's job to guard their children's privacy and protect them from well-meaning people who ask far too many questions. It should go without saying that a child should never be used as a public negative illustration, be demeaned, or be ridiculed in any way.

Respect is the foundation of all healthy relationships and crucial to the connection we make with our children—because kids actually are people.

## Accidents Will Happen (Grace)

Children make mistakes, as do young people, young adults, and supposedly mature adults. The *Encarta Dictionary* defines a mistake as "an incorrect act or decision," an "error," or a "misunderstanding."[6] Distinguishing between childish carelessness or mistakes and willful disobedience is important in child-rearing years. This little phrase, "Accidents will happen!" was used on numerous occasions to convey to our children that a childish mistake could easily be cleaned up or corrected—with no sense of shame or parental anger.

As parents, we want our children to not cover over their mistakes or excuse them, but rather to learn from them. As they grow, they need to "put away childish things" (1 Corinthians 13:11). With our help, they can do so, but it all needs to be covered by grace.

Grace, in spiritual terms, is defined as the unmerited favor of God. We, as sinful creatures, do not deserve—in any measure—the kindnesses of God. Yet He showers us with His goodness and mercy through the gift of salvation and the gift of His indwelling Spirit. Donald Sloat puts it this way, "Grace is a fundamental element of Christianity that permeates the Christian life."[7] In other words, since God has so generously bestowed grace upon us, we must in turn bestow it on others, especially our children.

There is a tension in every area of life regarding grace and the law, especially when raising children. When do you excuse an offense and offer another chance? Is there a limit? When do you stand firm in order to make a child understand his or her poor judgment or disobedience? A biblical parenting philosophy, guided by the wisdom of the Holy Spirit and wise counsel, will help parents discern the right response to those kinds of questions. My point here is that if we want our children to grow into men and women who know how to show grace to others, we must show it to them ourselves. And we certainly want them to give grace to us in the future!

A large part of our responsibility to our children involves discipline. I would not want anyone to misunderstand what I am saying—that I think we only give grace to our kids in the sense of excusing them. Part of that grace is their training, walking beside them and teaching them every single day. In Ephesians 6:4, Paul exhorts Christian parents to bring up their children "in the training and admonition of the Lord." The word *training*, from the Greek *paideia*, carries the idea of complete training and education of the child. I like the way *Thayer's Lexicon* puts it: "the cultivation of minds and morals."[8] The second word of verse 4, *admonition*, is from the Greek *nouthesia*, which relates to correction, admonition, and exhortation. I think we can surmise that the two words Paul chose to instruct parents pretty much say all we need to know. The challenge comes in consistently implementing teaching, training, and, if needed, appropriate punishment.

When our younger daughter Holly went to college, she had her first real car wreck, which ended up being a lifelong lesson in grace. She remembers it this way:

> One rainy day in Fort Worth I rear-ended someone while I was messing with the radio. Not only did I get in an accident, but I totaled the car and it was my fault! But much more than that, I remember the long drive to Dallas two days later with my mom and not knowing what Dad was going to say or if he would be disappointed in me. As I turned the corner onto our street, there in the driveway sat a shiny red Jeep Cherokee. Confused but intrigued, we pulled in behind it, and he walked outside to meet me.
>
> That day my dad taught me the best lesson in grace I have ever received. He said that just as I messed up and did not deserve a newer, nicer car than I had before, in the same way we do not deserve the infinite, merciful grace of Jesus. And as he handed me the keys, he told me that from that point on, every time I saw a red Jeep Cherokee it would be a picture of God's grace to me— and it is to this day!

As I stood in the kitchen witnessing this show of mercy, I wryly noted to myself that it was fortunate for Holly that she caught her dad on a good day. However, lessons on grace are not quickly forgotten, especially if they involve a new car and a loving and wise dad.

In the PK world, judgment often trumps grace. Not everyone is as generous and understanding of your children as you and your husband are, and like it or not, they are often unfairly judged. I remember getting a note once from a lovely woman in one of our churches who had worked with our daughter Wendy in one of our Christmas pageants. She expressed to me how much she enjoyed being around Wendy, how hard she had worked and how much fun she was. Then the zinger: "I always just assumed that the pastor's children were spoiled and rebellious. I am so happy to see that is not the case with Wendy." I guess the jury was still out on Holly, as far as she was concerned. The surprising thing to me was that her expectations for PKs were so negative. Somebody set the bar very low in her past experience.

As we give grace to our children, we pray that they will learn to give grace to others, especially church members that cross the boundaries or say ridiculous things to them. I have learned that people will say something to the pastor's wife that they don't have the nerve to say to the pastor. They will say to the pastor's kids what they don't have the nerve to say to his wife. At our house, we call these people "comment makers." They make offhand snide or sarcastic remarks under the guise of humor or teasing. If you react defensively or coolly, they will quickly laugh it off. "Just kidding!" We know that under these remarks are negative attitudes that just can't help being expressed. Helping children and young people handle these issues with grace and humor is invaluable. Helping them learn to laugh about the craziness of ministry life and refusing to take things too personally is an indirect way of giving grace. Being the recipient of God's grace enables us to give it to others and teach our children to do the same. "Blessed are the merciful, for they shall obtain mercy" (Matthew 5:7).

## Proud to Be Your Dad and Mom (Self-esteem)

"Proud to be your dad!" How many times has my husband written those words to his children in notes, birthday cards, or e-mails? It is his standard closing and illustrates another vital principle in raising emotionally healthy children—building their self-esteem and sense of security. I honestly have to say that outside of spiritual instruction related to a child's salvation and spiritual education, I think this is one of the most vital things parents can do to prepare their children for an emotionally mature adulthood.

Proverbs 17:6 says, "Children's children are the crown of old men, and the glory of children is their father." This verse indicates a child's built-in need for the parents' attention and approval. I am convinced that if children miss this element in early childhood, they will spend the rest of their lives looking for it. (That same thing goes for unconditional love, which is closely related to self-esteem.)

Developing a sense of security in a child is directly related to how the parents relate to him or her. A preschool teacher told me once that we should always tell our children that we are proud of them, especially when they do something obedient, thoughtful, or well. We should then add, "Aren't you proud of yourself?" This instills in them the satisfied feeling of receiving parental approval and attention.

The most helpful information I ever received on this topic was from Dr. Dobson's book *Hide or Seek*. After reading it carefully, I immediately implemented the principles he suggested. I instinctively knew this was truth, and I needed to listen closely to this Christian psychologist's good and godly counsel.

This book posits that in our culture, we assign the highest value of worth to those who have beauty and/or brains.[9] (I would add to that a third—athletic ability.) When we express our approval to a child, we often say, "You are so pretty!" or "You are so smart!" However, there is an inherent problem with that approach. No child can control if he or she is born with beauty, brains, or both. When we praise those conditions, it has little effect on reinforcing the child's behavior because it references something over which he or she has no control. I would not suggest that complimenting a child on looks or brains is a bad thing to do (and I do it all the time with my grandchildren), but there is a *better* thing to do. Dobson sees it this way: as our children grow, we are constantly teaching them to make good choices in all areas of their life.[10] Therefore, it makes more sense to compliment them on something very specific, such as "Thank you for feeding the dog without me asking you." When you give that kind of approval, you are noticing something the child chose to do, something he or she can control. These kinds of specific compliments just carry more weight than something more general.

Doing this successfully requires the rewording of the language of normal praise. Rather than saying, "You look pretty today," it's more effective to say, "You did your hair so well!" or "That's a good outfit you put together!" I tried this concept out years ago when we had some good family friends, the Amads, visit us for a weekend. They had an energetic and bright, little six-year-old boy who got underfoot a little when we were all in the kitchen preparing our sumptuous Palestinian dinner. I decided to experiment with this idea and gave him some specific jobs to do, always remembering to praise him for how well he did them. I loved his response! He could not do enough for us, would wait for his next task, and would wait in front of me for my smile and praise. When we sat down to dinner, his father nudged him over to my chair, motioning for him to pull out the chair for me, which he did. I made a big deal over that, and that's pretty much all we did the rest of the night. I would find an excuse to leave the table and he would jump up, nearly knocking his own chair over to quickly pull out my chair when I returned. His reaction confirmed that this approach was very effective! It's a small thing, but I have learned that incorporating this principle regarding compliments and praise is not only useful with children, but it is also very appreciated by adults.

Affirming children's interests, their gifts, their efforts, their be-havior—all of these things establish a strong sense of self-worth. When a child hears a parent's praise, that praise satisfies a deep emotional need and eventually helps the child transition into being a secure adult with a sense of self-respect and worth. That sense of security underlies every decision and relationship children have in the future. Children's hunger for approval, which builds their self-esteem, is met when parents intentionally give their children praise in a appropriate and thoughtful ways.

PKs are especially vulnerable to feeling unworthy. If they hear criticism of their parents and the church, it is inevitable that they will take it personally. Unfortunately, they hear criticism directed toward them and their parents much more than most other chil-dren do, which is not a good thing. Our family was always blessed with teachers and youth workers that usually took a special inter-est in our children. Their encouragement and friendship with our girls made them feel valued. I always saw these other adults as re-inforcing the sense of security we were trying to communicate. I encourage you to look for other authority figures in the lives of your PKs—such as teachers, coaches, or parents of friends—who can also provide the affirmation your children need.

### It Takes So Little to Be above Average (Pursue Excellence)

Years ago I had the opportunity to attend one of Florence Lit-tauer's CLASS seminars on developing leadership and speaking skills. While I knew I would be challenged and inspired, I had no idea I would come home with a little phrase that would quickly be incorporated forever into our family life. Florence spoke on the topic of her recent book, *It Takes So Little to Be Above Average.*[11] This little saying illustrated a couple of important principles of life, the first being how important it is to pursue excellence in every-thing we do. She challenged us to think above average, lead above average, care above average, and pray above average, just to name a few. Her premise was that most of the world settles for the mediocre in life. As Christians, through the power of the Spirit, and motivated by our desire to serve God, we should pursue excellence in our careers, family life, friendships, ministry, and everything else. Surely our service to Christ deserves nothing less.

The second principle this phrase illustrates is making the effort to "go the second mile," a phrase used by Jesus in the Sermon on the Mount (Matthew 5:41, paraphrase). During New Testament times, Roman soldiers had the right to force civilians into service by requiring them to carry their loads for them for one mile. In this sermon, Jesus is illustrating the principle of doing more for someone than the law requires. "Going the second mile" is a word picture of someone carrying a soldier's load further than the law requires. Paul refers to this same principle in Romans 12:9–21, in describing Christian behavior as "not lagging in diligence, fervent in spirit, serving the Lord" (v. 11).

This idea challenged me personally, and it soon became a mantra around our house, especially in the area of schoolwork. When doing a report, school project, or something for church, we would inevitably end up asking ourselves, "Is this above average?" Does this show that I have made an extra effort to do well? Whether or not a teacher, for example, would recognize this effort was not even that important. What *was* important was giving 100 percent of your effort to a project. I must add that I used this little phrase for myself as much as for my children. I am about as far from a perfectionist as anyone can be, so this little phrase was helpful in pushing me toward making extra efforts in everything I did. Whether parenting or teaching a Bible study (or even giving showers or entertaining), I became mindful of the importance of pursuing excellence in it all. While I know that I often failed to be above average, or even fell below average, I certainly did better in these areas than I would have otherwise.

When our children were growing up, we had a little dachshund named Rags. Many of our memorable family experiences have to do with the adventures of Rags, the little dachshund that envisioned himself as a two-hundred-pound German shepherd on hunting escapades in the forests of northern Germany. Personally, I had a love/hate relationship with the dog. He was not well behaved (that's the nicest way to put it), and he frequently annoyed me with his barking, getting into the trash, and doing all the things dogs do. During those times I would get irritated with him and scold him. He would sit perfectly still, look up at me with those brown eyes, cock his little head to one side, and his tail would barely twitch. I couldn't help but laugh and remind myself that his naughty behavior was a direct result of my not taking the time to train him when he came to live with us.

When Holly was in middle school, one of her courses was Spanish. She had a project due, and rather than making the typical poster, we decided to be *above average* and do a pretty fruit basket, attaching the names of the fruits in Spanish to each piece of fruit. The plan was that after the project was graded, she was to give the fruit basket to the teacher (this would be a good political move, according to her older sister). Holly worked hard on that basket, arranging the cards and fruit, and finally labeling it *"La Canasta de Frutas."* She carefully lettered each Spanish word on a pretty card and attached each one to the fruit with a decorative pin. Finally we had a lovely Above Average Fruit Basket ready to go and placed it on our dining room table.

The next morning when I came downstairs, I noticed an apple core by the stairs. It didn't take long for me to suspect Rags of doing something destructive, which was his specialty. Somehow during the night he had smelled that fruit and managed to jump up on a chair, pull the basket to the floor, and eat most of the fruit. The dining room floor was littered with banana peels, orange peels, peach pits and skin, grape stems . . . everything! Holly and I stood forlornly staring at the remains of the Above Average *La Canasta de Frutas*, with Rags right beside us—cocked head and all. I finally said to her, "Holly, you are probably the only person in history who can truthfully say, 'The dog ate my homework!'" As I recall, we quickly put another basket together, but it certainly would not have qualified as above average. I added an addendum to our saying that day—"when possible." No matter how hard you try, sometimes things end up as average, and that's OK. At least you tried!

O. S. and I worked to incorporate this principle in the lives of our PKs, especially in practicing manners and developing relationships. They were blessed to have the opportunities of frequently meeting other ministry leaders and having them in our home. Teaching a child to look an adult in the eye and answer polite questions appropriately is above average. Always speaking when spoken to is above average. Writing prompt thank-you notes is above average. Doing an extra thoughtful act (also known as a "random act of kindness") or expressing appreciation to someone when it's not required or expected is above average. This principle, I believe, serves any person well throughout life. Whether it's during college years, or while establishing a home, raising children, entering the workforce, showing hospitality, or anything else, learning to think above average pushes us toward excellence. It takes extra thought, extra energy, and extra planning, but it is worth it.

Paul illustrates this principle in Colossians 3:23–24: "And whatever you do, do it heartily, as to the Lord and not to men, knowing that from the Lord you will receive the reward of the inheritance; for you serve the Lord Christ." If we want to work and live "as to the Lord," then we will give it our all, since we do these things in service to Him.

*Always Remember Something . . . (Unconditional Love)*

Somewhere during the years of raising children, this phrase began to be repeated when we dropped our children off somewhere or left for a trip. The entire phrase was this: "Always remember something: I love you very much." Since children, especially older ones, tend to squirm when their parents gush about their love for them in front of others, we began to just use the first part of this phrase. Others may not have understood what our girls were supposed to "always remember," but Wendy and Holly certainly did. It was our code for saying, "Don't ever forget that we love you."

The need for unconditional love is the most primary of human emotional needs. This love is very close to the need for parental approval, as previously discussed. However, there is a difference. Children will inevitably do things that don't please parents and those will need to be addressed. But that never changes the fact that we love them, accept them as they are, and will always seek the best for them.

> *T*HE NEED FOR unconditional love is the most primary of human emotional needs.

In Isaiah 49:15, God was speaking to His people through the voice of His prophet Isaiah, reminding them that He had not forgotten them. "Can a woman forget her nursing child, and not have compassion on the son of her womb? Surely they may forget, yet I will not forget you." What a stunning statement of love. God uses an illustration of one of the most powerful forces of nature—maternal love and care—to describe the intensity of His love for His people. Of course it is a rhetorical question; can a mother forget her nursing baby? Absolutely not, it's unthinkable. But God says even if she did, He would never forget His chosen people. The relationship of God with the nation of Israel illustrates the ultimate in unconditional love. While they failed Him time and time again, He continued to forgive, discipline, and draw them back to Himself.

In their classic book, *The Blessing,* John Trent and Gary Smalley explore this concept, fleshing it out within a biblical context. This blessing is used to "communicate parental love and acceptance."[12]

There are five parts of the family blessing: meaningful touch, the spoken message, attaching "high value" to the one being blessed, picturing a special future for him or her (destiny), and a strong commitment to fulfill this blessing.[13] All of these convey a parent's unconditional love for the child in various ways. If the child recognizes and feels this love, he or she will inevitably pass it on to the next generation. But when children don't recognize their parents' unconditional love, they can have issues down the road. After all, as author P. D. James once said, "What a child doesn't receive, he can seldom later give."[14]

The important thing to realize is that even though all parents love their children, a child may not perceive it. This is surely one of the great mysteries of children. Their little minds often come up with conclusions that never entered the parents' thoughts at all. It is essential, therefore, that we learn to express our unconditional love in ways that cannot be misunderstood.

In the final chapter of their book, Trent and Smalley emphasize how parents' everyday interactions with their children express their love. During their seminars on this topic, the authors asked those who attended this question: "What is one specific way you knew that you had received your parents' blessing?"[15] I thoroughly enjoyed reading the responses; they were so touching. Take a look at some examples.

- "My parents really listened to me when I talked to them by looking directly into my eyes."
- "They would take each of us out individually for a special breakfast with Mom and Dad."
- "My mother always carried pictures of us in her purse." (Grandmothers, take note.)
- "My parents wouldn't change things in my bedroom without asking me."
- "Even when I was overweight in high school, my parents made me feel I was attractive."

- "My father would ask to talk to each of us kids personally when he called in from a trip."
- And this one is my favorite: "My father went with me when I had to take back an ugly dress a saleswoman had talked me into buying."[16]

These are small things, but notice how these small things left a lasting impression. And you can be sure that these respondents will eagerly pass down the blessing they received to their own children.

As a young mom and ministry wife, I remember a story that Johnnie Lord told during a parenting seminar. Her husband, Peter, pastored the Park Street Church in Titusville, Florida, in those days, and he was in great demand on the speaking circuit. Peter and Johnnie had five kids, and Johnnie remained at home most of the time in order to keep the family running smoothly. According to her, she began to notice that one of her daughters began to act lethargic and quiet. Her appearance became unkempt, and her usual good grades began to slip. Johnnie began to pray that God would give her "a window into her daughter's heart" (a phrase I have never forgotten) in order to see what was going on in her mind. As Johnnie prayed, she began to sense that she needed to spend some extra time with this child and see if she could draw out her feelings. As she did, she was surprised to learn that this daughter had concluded that her parents did not love her as much as they did her siblings. When Johnnie asked her specifically why, she really couldn't give an answer. All she knew was how she felt. Johnnie determined that the time pressures and stresses of their ministry home unintentionally had taken their time and attention away from this daughter. By purposely finding small ways to give her special attention and care, Johnnie and Peter saw her slowly return to her true self.

I have always remembered this story for two reasons. One, I love the idea of praying for a "window" into a child's heart in order to understand what he or she is thinking. Secondly, so often hurts can be eased and a child can be reassured in practical, everyday expressions of love. It's a cliché, but true nevertheless: how does a child spell love? T-I-M-E. Time spent together communicates love in a way that nothing else can.

Despite our failures, God is so good to honor the motives of parents' hearts. We must trust Him to bring our children along in His ways and do all we can to lead the way.

*Reflection*

◆ Which of the stressors Tracy Osborne identified could be troubling your children right now?

◆ Think of some of your own family sayings. What do they communicate?

◆ Think back on your own family of origin. How were you shown or not shown unconditional love and approval?

◆ How do you intentionally show respect, unconditional love, and approval to your children?

# 4

# The Friendship Connection:
## Sharing Your Life

When I was growing up, my extended family would often get together at my grandparents' home for dinner. After eating and cleaning up, we would all move into their living room where an upright piano with yellowed keys stood. My mom, an accomplished pianist, played while everyone sang old familiar songs, usually starting off with "The Eyes of Texas." (We have deep roots in central Texas; what do you expect?) I feel like I am describing a scene out of a corny movie, but I assure you these sing-alongs actually occurred. My dad's younger brother Joe and sister Carol always sang their famous rendition of the old classic "Side by Side." I doubt if anyone enjoyed it as much as they did, harmonizing and hamming it up for their audience as if they were performing on the *Ed Sullivan Show*. But I always loved the words to that old song because they describe companionship, whether a married couple, a parent and child, or two friends. One line of the song goes like this: "But we'll travel the road, sharin' our load, side by side."[1]

These words are not eloquent, but they speak to the simple joy of walking "side by side" with a companion on the journey of life. Scripture emphasizes the blessings of friendship. "A friend loves at all times, and a brother is born for adversity" (Proverbs 17:17). "The sweetness of a man's friend gives delight by hearty counsel" (Proverbs 27:9). "Better is a neighbor nearby than a brother far away" (Proverbs 27:10). Or as someone put it, "One loyal friend is worth ten thousand relatives." The examples of faithful friendship between Jonathan and David in the Old Testament and Mary and Elizabeth in the New Testament illustrate the beauty of two friends who love and encourage each other.

## The Necessity of Friendship

Ministry wives are particularly in need of supportive friendships, due to the many stresses and strains of their lifestyle. Being married to a pastor, staff member, or ministry leader does, however, bring some complications to the friendship connection. Who can you trust? How transparent can you be? How do you find a good friend who can keep a confidence? What do you do with loneliness? These are all very pertinent questions that deserve answers. Hopefully the conversation regarding friendship in this chapter will help clarify some of these issues.

Another common dilemma for ministry wives in developing friendships is serving in an area of the country that is rural with a small population. Many times those kinds of communities are more or less closed to "newcomers"—even if you have been there ten years. Such is the case with one of my young friends whose husband pastors in a small town. She told me that one of the primary challenges she and her husband face is finding ways to creatively pursue relationships with people, yet not take it personally when those pursuits don't yield much. They have struggled to find a support system, but with the busy schedule of other ministry couples in the area, there just isn't much time for developing friendships as couples or individuals. I met with some women a number of years ago at a pastors' conference in northern Colorado. I was dismayed to hear that most of them lived at least two hours away from any other ministry family, which contributed to their sense of isolation and loneliness.

I understand feeling alone in a church with no one the same age with whom to relate. In 1972, when I was twenty-one and my husband was all of twenty-four, we moved to Hobart, Oklahoma, where he became pastor of First Baptist Church. Hobart was a farming community in southwestern Oklahoma, a perfect example of "small-town America," with one stoplight. It was fun for us to walk into any store or one of the three restaurants in town and be greeted by name. Barbara Sue Guthrie, who worked the counter at her family's drugstore, Boothe Drugs, would start making one of her famous chocolate milkshakes for us the minute she saw one of us enter the store. She never asked if we wanted one; she just handed it to us with a big smile when we left.

The people in Hobart were absolutely wonderful to us, and we loved the years we spent in southwestern Oklahoma. However, when we arrived, there were few young couples in the town, and there were none in the church. That summer I had agreed to teach the young married women's Sunday school class. Imagine my surprise when I found out that the youngest woman in the class was twenty-eight, and she had three children! All of the women were around that age, and I was painfully aware of my inexperience in teaching women, and teaching in general. Nevertheless, I gave it my best shot, and I did all I knew to do—to just stick with the Scripture and not give too much commentary.

I was thrilled when a few months later our church called Rob and Kathy Gandy to serve with us. Rob was primarily our worship leader, but he also worked in every other area of the church, as many staff members in small churches do. Kathy was my age, and it was a blessing from God for us to have their friendship and camaraderie. The Gandys had a two-year-old son, Ken, and both of us had daughters who were born within a couple of weeks of each other. We worked hard to find other young couples in Hobart, and we were blessed to see a number of them join our fellowship. However, I have never forgotten how strange it felt to not have one friend near my own age in our community.

I once heard Jill Briscoe speak to a group of ministry wives on the topic of friendships. The conventional wisdom on this topic was (and to some extent still is) that a pastor's wife (or staff wife) is better off not having friends within the church, due to church members' jealousy or the appearance of favoritism. Jill, in her usual thoughtful way, explored this idea. She noted that Jesus had twelve companions that He called His friends (John 15:15). Of the twelve, three were in Jesus' inner circle—Peter, James, and John. She pointed out the fact that Jesus had close friends and this is one of the many ways we see His humanity. Everyone needs friends; God simply wired us that way. Jill then probed further: Did these close friendships sometimes cause problems in the larger group? Yes, at times they did (see Mark 10:41). Did it stop Jesus from having this inner circle? No. Conclusion: Human needs are more important than petty jealousies.

I found Jill's honest approach to the topic of developing friendships in a church or ministry quite refreshing. If Jesus Himself needed friends, why in the world would anyone, especially someone in ministry, think they could do without companionship? Friendship enables us to walk alongside others and share our burdens with them, and vice versa.

## The Ties That Bind

There is nothing that binds two people together more quickly than shared experiences. I can quickly name the common ground

I share with just about every single friend—or group of friends—I have. C. S. Lewis said, "Friendship is born at that moment when one person says to another, 'What! You, too? Thought I was the only one.'"[2] Of course, this is why ministry wives are especially needful of friends. Finding someone who shares your world and doesn't need complex explanations is truly a gift from God. The deepest friendships we develop are rooted in our shared faith and our journey on this earth. While we may have good friends who do not share these experiences, the bond between two believers is especially meaningful.

My husband and I spent fifteen wonderful years at First Baptist Church of Fort Lauderdale, Florida. When we moved there, our children were ages four and two. A few other moms who had children the same age quickly befriended me. However, it was the spiritual connection I found with a couple of those women that provided me with prayer support and close friendship at the time. We were just beginning an evangelism program (Evangelism Explosion), and as I was a trainee, I was required to pray with my two prayer partners once a week. Darla and Rita agreed to be my prayer partners, and we would sit at my kitchen table, praying for God to strengthen our EE teams and provide opportunities for us to share the gospel. After our prayer time, the coffeepot would come out and then the conversation and laughter would start in earnest.

Ministry in church life in general creates camaraderie and a sense of teamwork. Working together, worshiping together, and living in community bind our hearts to one another in an extraordinary way. A huge advantage (although I suppose there are those who would see it as a disadvantage) of church ministry is that it involves the whole family. PKs know staff members, deacons, and church leadership. They see what their parents do at least once a week on Sundays, and they have the opportunity to be active in the life of the church. I don't know of any other profession that allows for family involvement as much as church ministry. The connection that is developed with the church includes the entire ministry family.

Our church in Fort Lauderdale had a women's Bible study on Thursday mornings, which was a priority in my weekly schedule. I loved the fellowship of the women, the shared prayer requests, the excellent teaching—all of it. Seeking to practically apply scriptural principles to our marriages and young children, our hearts were quickly bound together. As our children grew, my circle of friends did also.

When our daughter Wendy was in middle school, I began to help in the youth ministry. Somehow the entertainment at retreats and camps seemed to fall to me and my friends Darla and Jan. Looking back on it, I don't think that was because we were unusually clever. I suspect it was because we were the only people asked to help who said yes. We would sit at a local diner writing skits and song parodies for hours, laughing uproariously and amusing ourselves with our own brilliance. I'm not sure others appreciated our efforts as much as we thought they should, but our shared experiences in youth ministry built lasting friendships—not to mention numerous inside jokes.

In my current stage of life, I share a special bond with my friends who are also grandmothers. We understand that showing pictures is mandatory, that telling adorable stories about our adorable grandchildren is always appropriate, and we instantly feel one another's pain when difficulties inevitably come along.

I also enjoy a group of friends based on our common interests. Kay, Dianne, and I all returned to school as adults to earn master's degrees. We decided several years ago to continue our education by reading books that are out of our box—that stimulate our thinking—and then discussing them. Proverbs 27:17 says, "As iron sharpens iron, so a man sharpens the countenance of his friend." We explore the edges of Christian thought, and we have read and discussed everything from goddess worship to the medieval mystics to pacifism to the emergent church. Our discussion times find us armed with books, markers, reading glasses, and, of course, good coffee. These friendships have deepened over the last few years as we share our own faith journeys and seek to understand, if not agree with, alternate points of view.

I use these examples to illustrate what I mean when I say that we develop friendships out of common interests. One of my young ministry wife friends told me that in her church her deepest friendships are with two older women. While they are not in the same stage of life, they share the same concerns and interests. It is nice to have friends of the same age, but sometimes our most meaningful relationships are formed with women that we would never have expected to be potential friends.

## Share Your Heart, but Use Your Head

One of the skills in developing and maintaining lasting friendships is finding the balance between being transparent and being appropriate. Allison, whose husband pastors a new church plant, puts it this way, "Even though we spend time with families in our church, they mostly see me through the lens of 'the pastor's wife.' It can be lonely at times. There is a thin veil between us and them with intimacy levels." I like her phrase, "a thin veil." Discerning how much transparency is appropriate is vital in maintaining healthy friendships.

There are plenty of topics to talk about: cultural issues, children, family dynamics, sports, politics, shopping, and a hundred other general interests women share. However, a ministry wife needs to always use discernment in disclosing personal information. I once heard a pastor's wife give good advice in this area. She suggested that a wife never share anything with someone in her church that she wouldn't want repeated. That is a good starting point. As relationships develop, you learn who can be trusted and who can keep a confidence. One thing is for certain, if a person discusses other people and their business with you, you can be 100 percent sure that she will discuss you with others as well.

If you do have a close friend in the church, it is a good idea to cultivate that friendship during the week. It is not wise to sit with one person exclusively or to carry on in-depth one-on-one conversations with her during time at church. Like it or not, perception is everything. Spend time with your friends as you wish during the week, but make an effort to get to know your church members while at church. I call this "spreading cheer and goodwill." There is something about the dynamics of going out of your way to speak to people and visit with them that communicates that you care.

There are two ironclad rules that I suggest. First, never share something with a church member that would affect how she would view your husband in the pulpit. Never say something about him that would prevent someone from hearing from the Holy Spirit as he preaches or teaches God's Word. Second, never discuss "church business" such as finances, staff relationships, or confidential matters. Debbie, a wise friend of mine, puts it this way, "I have learned to be a little more guarded to protect the integrity of my husband, our marriage, and his ministry." If there are serious emotional, familial, or marital issues that need to be addressed, a friend or close relative outside of the church is usually the best resource.

## You've Got a Friend . . . Somewhere

Ministry wives frequently mention loneliness as one of their most difficult challenges. Spend an hour roaming through ministry wives' blogs and you will hear it over and over again—"I'm lonely. I really need a friend or two." Sometimes it seems like there are two extremes found in church relationships. A woman may either be kept at arm's length (as in a closed community) by the other women in the church or pursued relentlessly by women she has zero interest in knowing.

A few years ago I was invited to speak to a group of ministry wives in a small community outside of Dallas. I had previously met the pastor's wife who was organizing this event, and I was impressed with her energy and interest in developing friendships among ministry wives in her area. This group of eight to ten women, from diverse church affiliations, met monthly for a casual dinner and conversation. While I was prepared to speak to these women (the reason I was invited), once we began to eat and visit, I quickly realized that they didn't need much urging to interact. We covered our topic, and then I sat back and watched them minister to one another. One of the women and her husband had just recently retired from their church, and she was praying for God to show her what He had for her to do in this new stage of life. At the other end of the spectrum was a young wife who had recently delivered twins. She was trying to figure out how to manage twins, a new church plant, and a husband who was still in seminary. Plus, she needed to return to work for financial reasons. As I watched their interaction, I thought, "This is what every ministry wife needs—a group of trusted friends who understand her world and will support her as she struggles to figure it all out." I was energized after meeting with these women and encouraged by their commitments to their husbands and their churches, as well as their genuine friendships with each other.

Thankfully today we have the Internet with numerous websites and blogs that address the needs of the ministry wife and family. Focus on the Family has a plethora of articles and interviews regarding ministry, as does the Global Pastors Network and LifeWay Christian Resources. These websites and others provide an online community for wives and children of ministers.[3] While researching for this book, I came upon the website www.preacherskids.com, which was founded as a support for ministry children. While there is no substitute for "someone with skin on," at least there are several venues for connecting with other women and ministry families.

How do you find friends? Proverbs 18:24 says, "A man who has friends must himself be friendly." About twenty years ago, one of my friends moved from Texas to South Carolina, where her husband accepted the position of pastor of the renowned First Baptist Church, Columbia. Being a spirited Texas girl who dressed with flair (and enjoyed wearing a cowboy hat at times), Lynda found that adjusting to the culture and church traditions of the Deep South was challenging. While everyone was very gracious and kind to her, she needed some "girlfriends." After reading and mulling over Proverbs 18:24, Lynda decided to try an experiment. For a few weeks she observed women in their church. She then chose five women whom she found interesting and thought she would like, and she invited them all to lunch at her home. Of course none of them knew why they were there. After the customary chit-chat, Lynda told the women frankly that she was lonely and needed friends. She had chosen them because she believed they all had something in common and could build friendships together. As you would expect, the women responded immediately, eager to be her friends. According to Lynda, those friendships led to other friendships, and so on and so on. I like this story because I admire Lynda for being so proactive. It is true that she had an advantage many women don't have, living in a metropolitan area where there are plenty of people to choose from. Nevertheless, she took a risky and creative approach to her need for friends. It certainly paid off.

If you find yourself in Lynda's stilettos, I suggest first finding a network of supportive women online at one of the many websites and blogs that are waiting at your fingertips. Taking a proactive approach may not always pay off as you might like, but you never know who God might be preparing to be your friend. I recently read an article by pastor's wife Cindy Dykes, who suggests that you concentrate on building relationships with your church leaders, such as staff, deacons, elders, or lay leaders.[4] These are people with whom you automatically share church interests, which is a good starting point.

## The Hospitality Connection

A book on ministry wives would not be complete without a conversation on hospitality. Opening your home and sharing what you have with others is an expression of love, acceptance, and friendship. While there is the personal connection, nothing develops friendship with church members in general as much as the hospitable home. However, demanding schedules today barely allow time at home together as a family, much less for guests. How does the Christian tradition of hospitality fit into the twenty-first century world?

The dictionary defines hospitality as a friendly and generous reception of guests or strangers.[5] But the root meaning and usages of the word give a fuller sense of its meaning. The latin *hospes* means "guest" or "host," and it is the basis for our words *hospice, hospital, host,* and *hotel,* among others.[6] You might notice that these words imply not only guest and host, but care and generosity as well.

Hospitality is listed as a requirement for church leadership—for those who shepherd the flock—in 1 Timothy 3:2 and Titus 1:8. There is a strong biblical tradition regarding this practice, which is rooted in Middle Eastern culture. The Old Testament gives numerous illustrations of hospitality shown to strangers, from Abraham and Sarah (Genesis 18:1–3) to the demands of the law (Deuteronomy 10:17–19) to the Shunammite woman who welcomed the prophet Elisha into her home (2 Kings 4:8–10). The New Testament exhorts Christians to be hospitable as well (Romans 12:13; 1 Peter 4:9; 3 John 8). The biblical tradition of hospitality is woven throughout the narratives of Scripture, and it even has theological implications. Christine Pohl writes:

> Images of God as gracious and generous host pervade the biblical materials. God provides manna and quail daily in the wilderness for a hungry and often ungrateful people. God offers shelter in a hot and dry land, and refreshment through living water. Israel's covenant identity includes being a stranger, an alien, a tenant in God's land—both dependent on God for welcome and provision and answerable to God for its own treatment of aliens and strangers.[7]

The New Testament portrays Jesus as an unwelcome guest (John 1:11) who was rejected by the very world He created. The fact that during the three years of His Galilean ministry He had no home of His own indicates that He must have frequently been the recipient of someone's hospitality.

> This intermingling of guest and host roles in the person of Jesus is part of what makes the story of hospitality so compelling for Christians. Jesus welcomes and needs welcome; Jesus requires that followers depend on and provide hospitality. The practice of Christian hospitality is always located within the larger picture of Jesus' sacrificial welcome to all who come to Him.[8]

Lauren Winner has written an interesting little book entitled *Mudhouse Sabbath*. As a former orthodox Jew and now a Christian, Winner discusses some of the Jewish rituals from the perspective of a Christian. One of these is the concept of hospitality, which according to Jewish tradition is of primary importance. She comments:

> In Hebrew, this is *hachnassat orchim*, literally "the bringing in of guests." Sociologists might suggest that Jews do hospitality so well because they have spent so many centuries being the stranger and the friendless ... Later rabbinic literature surrounds the biblical stories and models with codes and instructions. Rabbi Yochanan insisted that practicing hospitality was even more important than praying. Some rabbis turn hospitality into architecture, urging faithful Jews to build houses with doors on all four sides so that travelers and guests might find a welcome door from any direction. Many Jewish communities adopted the idea of serving all their dinner courses at once; this way finicky guests would not have to suffer through an appetizer or bowl of soup they did not like ...
>
> Early Christian communities continued these practices of hospitality, attempting to feed the poor, host travelers, visit the

imprisoned, invite widows and orphans to join them at meal-time—all expressions of a capacious notion of hospitality.[9]

These historical and biblical precedents help us grasp the deeper meaning of what it means to be hospitable. It differs from entertaining, which infers an emphasis on one's home, food presentation, and skill. True hospitality is more than that—much more. It includes not only caring for others' physical needs but their spiritual and emotional ones as well, which is the essence of friendship. And we should always remember the admonition in Hebrews 13:2, that some have entertained angels without realizing it. Matthew 25:31–46 is one of the primary texts that has formed the Christian view of hospitality and care. The command to serve "the least of these" (v. 45) has been a basic motivation for countless compassion-based ministries.

One of the best New Testament examples of hospitality is found in the story of Mary, Martha, and Lazarus, a small family in the village of Bethany, on the eastern slope of the Mount of Olives. Jesus was the recipient of their loving hospitality many times and had a close friendship with them as indicated in John 11:5. In Luke 10:38–42 there is the account of an incident that happened one day as Martha was busy preparing for their guests. Jesus was most likely very comfortable in their home, having frequently been the recipient of their hospitality. He was a welcomed guest and close friend, according to the passage. Martha was quite overwhelmed with her preparations, and she became irritated that Mary was so oblivious to all the work that needed to be done. Martha finally blurted out, "Lord, do You not care that my sister has left me to serve alone? Therefore tell her to help me" (Luke 10:40). Jesus' reply was a gentle rebuke. "Martha, Martha, you are worried and troubled about many things. But one thing is needed, and Mary has chosen that good part, which will not be taken away from her" (vv. 41–42).

I cannot count the number of sermons I have heard at conferences rebuking Martha for her lack of spiritual sensitivity and praising Mary for focusing her attention on Jesus. However, a careful reading of the text provides some detail about these sisters that one might miss. In verse 39, Luke makes a point to say that Martha had a sister named Mary, "who also sat at Jesus' feet and heard His word." The key word here is "also." Martha was a woman with spiritual depth, as was Mary. In fact, it is Martha who gives one of the most powerful confessions of faith in the New Testament in John 11:25–27, while standing at her brother Lazarus' grave. Martha had a crystal clear understanding of who Jesus was: "You are the Christ, the Son of God, who is to come into the world" (v. 27).

Martha's irritation with Mary was not because of a lack of spiritual depth. She was overwhelmed with her duties on this particular day and simply needed some help. The text says that she was "distracted," which means to be divided or pulled away; not only that, but she was "distracted with much serving" (Luke 10:40). It was too much work for her to do alone, despite her abilities. I have often sympathized with Martha when reading this passage. Like most women, I identify with her stress and frustration. I would be irritable too if thirteen men dropped in for lunch at my house! But that is no excuse. Jesus firmly reminded her that in her busyness, Martha had forgotten the most important thing of all—her guest! Mary had kept her focus on Jesus, despite the chaos and demands around her. There are many layers to this story, but for our purposes here, we see an all-too-familiar scenario. The main thrust of hospitality is not the food, table setting, or entertainment, but making a guest feel genuinely welcomed and comfortable.

We know that Martha fervently desired to serve the Lord (see John 12:2) and was a woman of great faith. Yet she missed the joy of true hospitality in this particular incident. "Be hospitable to one another without grumbling" (1 Peter 4:9).

Throughout church history, hospitality has been considered essential in creating Christian community. Early Christians believed that sharing meals and opening their homes to those with diverse backgrounds indicated that they truly were united in their faith.[10] Hospitality within the early church played a key role in the spreading of the gospel as well. When Paul and other preachers of the gospel and leaders of the church traveled the Mediterranean world, they often stayed for periods of time in the homes of other Christians, such as Lydia (see Acts 16:14–15). Can you imagine the dinner conversations that took place? I envision people sitting transfixed as Paul, Barnabas, Silas, or other missionaries related the miraculous stories of God's grace to their fellow believers.

Hospitality not only provided a place for worship services, shared meals, and fellowship, but more importantly it served as a way to promote unity and mutual respect among a culture of both rich and poor believers.[11] As the centuries passed, the tradition of a welcoming home or church eager to serve the members of its community remained a hallmark of the Christian witness.

Churches, as well as homes, should be a welcoming place. Our former church in Fort Lauderdale found a creative way to offer hospitality and develop a general friendship with our community. During the winter months, the population of south Florida always mushrooms. The "snowbirds" from the Northeast and Midwest arrive to warm weather, as do the homeless and destitute. As someone once told us, "If I have to live in my car, at least I won't freeze here like I would in Michigan."

First Baptist is located in the downtown area of the city, where many of the homeless camp out. Our church ministered to these needy people, regularly providing clothing and food for them. However, one year we decided to be more purposeful in our efforts to be hospitable to our community. My husband, O. S., had introduced the idea of the "Feast of Plenty" in a sermon he preached on Luke 14:12–14. In that passage Jesus taught a parable on humility, ending it with a challenge to his hosts.

> "When you give a dinner or a supper, do not ask your friends, your brothers, your relatives, nor rich neighbors, lest they also invite you back, and you be repaid. But when you give a feast, invite the

poor, the maimed, the lame, the blind. And you will be blessed, because they cannot repay you; for you shall be repaid at the resurrection of the just" (Luke 14:12–14).

Based on those words of Jesus, the Saturday before Thanksgiving that year we held our first annual "Feast of Plenty." The meal consisted of a full turkey and dressing meal served outdoors to hundreds (and eventually thousands) of people at no cost to them. We provided buses to transport people who lived in nursing homes or homes for the mentally disabled. Our parking lots and the main streets downtown were covered with tables and chairs, and hosts and hostesses would see that our guests were seated and served. After the meal, we had evangelistic preaching and singing, sharing the gospel any way we could. It took hundreds of our people to pull off this event, as you can imagine. Coordinating bus schedules, finding parking spaces, obtaining permits from the city, preparing for food arrival, cooking the turkeys, slicing the turkeys, child care—there were endless details to cover. But there is no way to put into words how our people loved that event. We always had plenty of workers at the feast, because we all found such joy in serving those less fortunate than ourselves. In fact, as the years passed, we often had so much food given to us by local restaurants and bakeries that we had to work overtime to be sure it was all eaten.

I remember on one occasion helping some elderly women off of a bus and escorting them to their table. I spotted one of our new church members (a prominent businessman) with a fragile, elderly woman in his arms, carrying her like a baby. As I drew closer to him, I noticed tears running down his face. I stopped and asked if everything was all right, to which he replied, "This little lady just told me how excited she was about being here today. She lives in a nursing home and hasn't been outside for three years." As a church family, we felt honored that God would entrust the ministry of hospitality to us and allow us to share our blessings with "the least of these." I tell this story to emphasize that hospitality does not just take place in individual homes, but in the shared ministry of the body of Christ.

> *I* ENCOURAGE ministry wives to see hospitality not as an obligation, but as a privilege.

My mother, as you might expect, is very gifted at hospitality. We often had extended family and guests in our home. Due to her influence, as a ministry wife I was very agreeable to opening our home to our church and community. Still, I discovered that there is a certain amount of intentionality in doing so. It takes time, energy, and usually some expense to have guests, not to mention detailed planning. However, there are thousands of books and websites that give excellent ideas regarding cost, recipes, and themes. Never before have women had so much help in this area. I have also learned that few people expect elaborate food preparation or expect to see a showcase home. They simply want to feel welcomed and enjoy the friendship with their hosts.

I encourage ministry wives to see hospitality not as an obligation, but as a privilege. And remember that "practicing" hospitality is simply that—practice. The very phrase reminds us that we never have our homes, table, or food perfect. We are simply opening our homes or churches in order to build connections in life, especially spiritual ones. Lauren Winner offers this realistic insight: "To be a hostess, I'm going to have to surrender my notions of *Good Housekeeping* domestic perfection. I will have to set down my pride and invite people over even if I have not dusted. . . . If I wait for immaculate, I will never have a guest."[12]

My purpose in this particular conversation has been to offer a larger perspective of hospitality within the context of friendship as part of our Christian tradition. Making time in our busy schedules to open our homes and offer comfort and sustenance to body and soul will take purposeful planning. But it is well worth the effort, and it reflects the loving nature of our Lord.

One of the shortest books in the New Testament is a letter written by the apostle Paul to his dear friend Philemon. The topic is Philemon's runaway slave, Onesimus, who had apparently robbed his master, Philemon, and then fled to Rome. While there, Onesimus had fallen under the preaching of Paul and had been converted to Christ. Paul's letter to Philemon is an appeal for Philemon to forgive Onesimus his offenses and to recognize their new spiritual relationship as brothers in Christ, as well as slave and master. Paul uses the word *refreshed* in reference to his friendship with Philemon. "For we have great joy and consolation in your love, because the hearts of the saints have been refreshed by you, brother" (Philemon 7). According to *Vines Expository Dictionary of New Testament Words*, the word *refresh* in Greek means "to give intermission from labor, to give rest."[13] Philemon's friendship ministered to Paul and his companions, bringing them a spiritual and emotional breather from their intense labors in the gospel.

Even the apostle Paul, who sometimes seemed superhuman, needed a friend. Philemon's love and friendship brought him joy, comfort and rest. What a simple, yet profound expression of the nature of true friendship—celebrating the joys of life together and consoling one another when troubles inevitably come. This is the friendship connection—"sharin' our load, side by side."[14]

## *Reflection*

◆ Colleen Evans, author and pastor's wife, suggests that if you have been unsuccessful at forming friendships, perhaps you should ask God to show you why. Ask yourself, "Am I willing to be transparent and trusting? Am I willing to give of myself? Am I willing to risk? And if I have been betrayed and wounded by a past friendship, am I willing to let God heal me so I can love and trust again?"[15]

◆ Are you cultivating friendships? Even if it is not possible to spend time together physically, we can strengthen our friendships through email, blogging, or phone calls.

◆ Have you ever considered hospitality as a spiritual act of service? As ministry wives it is helpful to see hospitality not as an obligation, but as creating an opportunity for friendships to develop. Christine Pohl says, "Hospitality thus emerges from a willingness to create time and space for people."[16] Sharing a meal or even a cup of coffee in a home environment creates a unique setting for strengthening relationships. Think of opening your home as a demonstration of God's grace and as a deliberate act of sharing your life with someone else. This adds a good balance to the work and energy hospitality usually requires. Don't let a lack of expertise in cooking or entertaining prevent you from finding joy in the spiritual practice of hospitality!

# 5

# The Church Connection:
## Relating to the Women in Your Church

*A*ll of the connections we have discussed so far are personal, such as husbands, children, and friends. However, there is also a "church connection"—the relationship the ministry wife has with her church as a whole, and the women in particular. This is one aspect of ministry that I have thoroughly enjoyed. I have been extremely blessed in my life with the presence of wonderful women. My mother was (and is) a superb role model in marriage and family life. I often say that she has always made my life easier (with the possible exception of my teenage years!). I also grew up with a great deal of interaction with my grandmothers and my aunts, whom I love dearly. All of that to say, I like women. Additionally, in every church we have served, I found older women who were interested in my life and reached out to befriend me. I have had excellent examples of Christian womanhood in my life, and I am forever in their debt.

The church is community, and community consists of relationships. Relating to and ministering with other women in kingdom work hopefully results in friendships and lasting influences, due to our common commitment to Christ. Dietrich Bonhoeffer, in his classic book *Life Together*, said, "Christianity means community through Jesus Christ and in Jesus Christ. Whether it be a brief, single encounter or the daily fellowship of years, Christian community is only this. We belong to one another only through and in Jesus Christ."[1] I have heard it said that (due to our common faith) often we are closer to our Christian brothers and sisters than we are to our own blood relatives. These relationships, then, take on added significance in the life of a Christian and especially in the life of a ministry wife.

Paul used the analogy of the human family to illustrate the nature of our relationships with other believers. He says in 1 Thessalonians 2:7, "But we were gentle among you, just as a nursing mother cherishes her own children"; 1 Thessalonians 2:11, "As you know how we exhorted, and comforted, and charged every one of you, as a father does his own children"; and 1 Thessalonians 4:6, "That no one should . . . defraud his brother in this matter [sexual immorality]." Using this analogy intensifies the importance of relationships within the church, raising them to the highest standard—familial love. Again in 1 Timothy 5:1–2 he says, "Do not rebuke an older man, but exhort him as a father, younger men as brothers, older women as mothers, younger women as sisters, with all purity." In Paul's letter to the Galatians he says, "Therefore, as we have opportunity, let us do good to all, especially to those who are of the household of faith" (Galatians 6:10). Esteeming, or honoring, the family of God in this way adds weight to the importance of our relationships with other women in the church. They are not just casual friendships, but relationships with eternal significance.

## A Pattern of Christian Womanhood

Titus 2:1–9 specifically addresses the social order of the church. Paul is pressing for believers to preserve respectability and maintain appropriate social structures, since godly behavior would protect the witness of the early church. He begins this chapter with an exhortation: "But as for you, speak the things which are proper for sound doctrine" (Titus 2:1). Along with the speaking or teaching, however, is the behavior of the Christian, which is addressed in the following verses. Paul lists specific characteristics that illustrate spiritual maturity and Christian ideals. He says, "In all things showing yourself to be a pattern of good works; in doctrine showing integrity, reverence, incorruptibility, sound speech that cannot be condemned" (Titus 2:7).

Numerous times in the New Testament believers are exhorted to be examples of the faith. The Greek word used here is *typos,* which means a pattern, a shape, or a model for imitation.[2] Public leaders wield great influence, and Paul recognized how important it was for church leadership to demonstrate to the unsaved world and to new believers how a follower of Christ lives, works, and relates to family and the world.

My mom is an excellent seamstress and enjoys sewing and creating lovely clothing, pillows, tablecloths . . . you name it. Her creative streak ranges from music to sewing to her green thumb. Growing up, I always marveled at how she could make anything—from an Ultrasuede overcoat to Austrian curtains—and relished doing so. She could closely examine a garment in a store (in the dressing room, of course), go straight home, and reproduce it to the smallest detail. She sewed most of my sister's and my clothing, which we appreciate now certainly more than we did then. Many of my memories are of my mother holding up a Simplicity or McCall's pattern to me, muttering to herself and consulting her tape measure. She knew that the accuracy of the pattern determined the outcome of the garment. If the pattern was too small, too big, or too ill-fitting, the garment would be as well. I must add here that my mother tried with all the strength she had to make me into a seamstress. Unfortunately I barely mastered the Jiffy pattern before I finally gave up. I can sew on a button and put in a hem, but that is the extent of my sewing skills. Fortunately the sewing gene showed up in one of my nieces, to the delight of my mom.

This visual is what Paul is referring to as a "model" or "pattern." It is a standard, a prototype of Christian womanhood (or manhood) that is lived out in front of people in order for them to imitate those very characteristics. Of course this is true in raising children—they usually model their parents. So it is in the body of Christ.

The pattern of the "older women" consists of certain characteristics. They are to show "reverent" behavior, which means they are to conduct themselves in an appropriate and honorable manner (Titus 2:3). They are not to be "slanderers," which means falsely accusing someone or spreading malicious gossip (v. 3). Nor is an older woman who is modeling Christian womanhood to be "given to much wine," meaning she exercises self-control and is not in bondage to any substance, and she is to teach "good things," such as loving your husband, loving your children, and making your home a priority (v. 3).[3]

There is another aspect of this passage that needs to be noted. There is room for interpreting the Greek words for "older" and "young" (Titus 2:3–4) as not necessarily referring to chronological age.[4] In other words, Paul could be encouraging the spiritually mature women to teach the new Christian women, irrelevant of their chronological ages. There is good support for that view, since Paul is exhorting women to demonstrate Christian characteristics that reveal spiritual maturity, not necessarily physical maturity. Honorable behavior, avoiding gossip, loving husbands and children, being industrious homemakers—all of these traits can be shown in a woman's life, no matter what her age.

Paul speaks to this very thing in his letter to his spiritual son Timothy. He says, "Let no one despise your youth, but be an example to the believers in word, in conduct, in love, in spirit, in faith, in purity" (1 Timothy 4:12). Once again, Paul's counsel to Timothy is to "be an example" by his words, actions, and spiritual maturity despite his age. This pattern of good works is to serve as an example to those whom God has entrusted to our spiritual care (see 1 Peter 5:2–3).

I have been blessed to have close friends in ministry, especially older women who provided this pattern for me. These women were my friends as well as mentors. Their examples influenced me every bit as much as their wise words. One of those women is Betty Jean Billingsley, whose husband, Bill, was a former pastor of Sheridan Hills Baptist Church in Hollywood, Florida. Since we lived in the same area (south Florida), I had the opportunity to frequently see Betty Jean and hear her speak. I loved to hear her share her insights in seminars or Bible studies, and I watched her demeanor and graciousness. Just thinking about her as I write these words brings a flood of appreciation for her investment in my life.

During one of those studies, Betty Jean reminded us that we must make every effort possible, especially as busy families in ministry, to stay emotionally connected to our children and find creative ways to do so. She told a story about her daughter Laura, who had just started babysitting. At that time one of the most popular television shows was *Little House on the Prairie*. The night it was on television, her daughter had a standing babysitting appointment. After Laura put the children to bed, she would call her mom and they would talk on the phone and watch the show together. I thought it was quite ingenious of Betty Jean to come up with this idea and determined that I would do exactly the same thing if I ever had the opportunity. Several years later, when Holly was a middle schooler, that opportunity came along and I took it. We would rush home from church on Wednesday night, pull out the chips and salsa, and sit on the sofa watching *The Wonder Years* together. I liked getting my fix of sixties music and memories almost as much as Holly liked watching young Fred Savage, who played Kevin. I doubt if we sat there one time when I did not think about

Betty Jean and Laura. Betty Jean's "pattern" gave me a specific illustration of finding a creative way to spend time with one of my
daughters.

## Learning by Observing

Proverbs 24:30–34 comments on the wisdom of learning by
observation. A man walked by the field of a lazy man and noticed
how it was overgrown with thorns and its fences were broken
down. He stopped to observe this scenario, and the Scripture
records him saying, "When I saw it, I considered it well; I looked
on it and received instruction" (v. 32). He continues with his conclusions after observing the field: "A little sleep, a little slumber, a
little folding of the hands to rest; so shall your poverty come like a
prowler, and your need like an armed man" (vv. 33–34). The point
of this short passage is twofold. It is primarily a warning about lazi-
ness and its inevitable results. But there is a secondary reflection—
the wisdom of learning by observation. Paul exhorted Christian
leaders in numerous New Testament passages to live exemplary
lives, so that others would see their example and do the same. The
strongest message we as ministry wives send is not so much our
wise words, but our living example of what it looks like to be a follower of Christ (see 1 Peter 3:2).

One of my friends, Janet Wicker, is the wife of Hayes Wicker,
pastor of First Baptist Church, Naples, Florida. Recently we were
together at a ministry wives event and Janet introduced Carol Ann
Draper, who had a part in the program. Carol Ann and her husband, Jimmy, are two of the most respected and loved people in
the Southern Baptist Convention. Jimmy pastored several churches
throughout his ministry, and he spent the last twenty years before
his retirement as president of LifeWay Christian Resources. In her
introduction, Janet told the story of how Carol Ann had influenced
her life without even realizing it by just being visible in the corporate worship service.

Janet is from a small town in Georgia, and she moved to Fort Worth, Texas, in 1974 to attend Southwestern Baptist Theological Seminary, in order to prepare for her call to ministry. At that time she had no interest in marrying a preacher, and she was determined not to do so (which of course she eventually did). She was preparing for the mission field or any other venue where she felt God leading. As seminary students, Janet and her friends attended First Baptist Church of Dallas. One Sunday, someone pointed out Carol Ann Draper, who was the wife of then associate pastor Jimmy Draper. Janet began to notice that Carol Ann always had an elderly woman with her and found out that it was Carol Ann's mother-in-law, whom everyone called "Grandmother." Carol Ann would enter the auditorium, get Grandmother comfortably settled and then greet those around her. She would give quick hugs or handshakes and make a little conversation, always with a smile on her face. Janet put it this way: When Carol Ann entered the auditorium, "the lights came on." She said:

> It was the example of Carol Ann Draper to this once young seminary student that God provided for me in my calling as the wife of a pastor. She had no idea I was watching her, but just through her living, godly example and her faithful presence in the church, I was blessed and taught. When Hayes and I took our first church, it was the picture of Carol Ann as a pastor's wife that I used as my standard. And after these many years, I still do.

I was very impressed with Janet's introduction of Carol Ann and later discussed her comments with her in more detail. I asked her what exactly she had determined from her observations. She thought it through and came up with these conclusions. First, Carol Ann genuinely cared about people. Her gentleness with Grandmother and her smiles and interaction with the congregation simply made people feel loved. She was approachable, spoke to people, and made them feel noticed and appreciated. Second, Carol Ann participated in the worship service. She clearly had a spiritual life. When the time for the sermon came, she opened her Bible and took notes. Third, she was faithful in her attendance of the corporate worship service. She was supportive of the church ministry and her husband's preaching ministry. These are very basic observations, true. But Janet and I agreed that if all one ever knew about being a ministry wife was from Carol Ann's example, then it would more than do. I join Janet in honoring an exemplary woman, Carol Ann Draper, who authentically lived out a "pattern of good works" before her people. I also commend Janet for having the good sense to notice Carol Ann and for having a teachable spirit.

I recently read the following comment, which helped me understand why even just speaking to people in our church family carries such weight. "Recognition involves respecting the dignity and equal worth of every person and valuing their contributions, or at least their potential contributions, to the larger community."[5] Perhaps just being purposeful in noticing others and making the effort to acknowledge them is more significant than we realize.

It's a fact that a large part of church leadership is just being visible. Like it or not, church members watch the ministry family. If the minister's wife and children have a degree of involvement in church life, it gives great credibility to the leadership of the minister. I am not speaking here of jobs or responsibilities that a wife might take on, but simply her presence in her church community. I personally believe it is vital, from a leadership standpoint, for a church body to see a ministry wife taking part in the corporate worship experience. Of course, this participation hopefully is based on her spiritual desire to live in community with the body of Christ, not just to please other people. This is a crucial point of leadership—not just talking, but doing. I believe this is what Paul was referring to in Titus 2:7: "In doctrine showing integrity," which is actually living out what we profess to believe.

In the same vein, a young ministry wife once told me, "I grew up in the church and with the pastor's kids, but none of the staff wives were very visible at church. So there was no model for me to follow when I married a minister." The thing that struck me regarding this comment was that she had missed just having someone to watch, as an example to follow. I would go so far to say that the ministry of just being visible and participating in corporate worship is a significant one and should not be dismissed lightly.

However, this brings up another issue. In past generations, the general understanding was that the pastor's wife had to be at church "every time the doors were open." It seems to me that the pendulum then swung to the opposite extreme, and in my generation we heard ministry wives say, "I don't work for the church; I don't have to be there if I don't want to be." I suggest that the best approach is found somewhere in the middle, as usual. While we certainly shouldn't rate our spiritual maturity or value by our attendance at church activities (which equates to legalism), nevertheless there is a balance that needs to be established. It is absolutely true that we have liberty in Christ—the liberty to obey Him and follow Him as He leads us. However, there are some accommodations that need to be made at times. It is a wise and spiritually perceptive woman who understands the value of providing a visual image of Christian womanhood for the women in her church. And even more importantly, it is a wise and spiritually perceptive woman who obediently follows Christ's command to do so.

## Learning by Being Taught

When our family moved to Ada, Oklahoma, in 1974, we looked forward to meeting the many young families in our congregation. We were immediately befriended by several of these couples, and it didn't take long to form deep friendships. Without a doubt, the foundation of these relationships was laid by Pete and Frances Cantrell, faithful church members of First Baptist, Ada. Everyone loved the Cantrells; they were full of life and enjoyed hosting a Bible study for young married people in their home one night a week. I can remember the laughter, the prayer, and the spiritual instruction we received from this couple who served us so faithfully . . . and seemed to thoroughly enjoy it all.

Frances was a skilled Bible teacher, but more than that, she had a heart for ministering the Word. She also taught a class on Wednesday morning for women, aptly named JOY Bible Study. Her instant friendship and genuine concern regarding our family and our spiritual well-being quickly endeared her to me. The JOY Bible Study became a weekly event in my life that I did not want to miss. It wasn't just the close fellowship, but also the spiritual intimacy we shared as a group of women, that planted a desire in my heart to seek the Lord in a way I never had before. In the power of the Spirit, and armed with her Scofield Bible, Frances taught on the life of Moses that year. I was absolutely mesmerized by her teaching. I was unfamiliar with the "types"[6] in the Old Testament, and the richness of biblical truth in the way she taught it was life-changing to my friends and me. On top of that, Frances was a real prayer warrior—a term I do not use lightly. She knew how to pray and taught us to do so as well. As in every church, there were some heart-wrenching things that happened that year, and Frances taught the JOY Bible Study women how to pray and intercede according to Scripture.

One day during that winter, one of our daughters was sick and I was unable to go to Bible study. Frances called me early that morning, and I glumly told her I couldn't be there and would be cleaning out a kitchen cabinet, which desperately needed it. She laughed her contagious laugh and said, "Honey, go read Colossians 3:17. It's not any more spiritual to go to Bible study than it is to take care of your children and clean out your cabinets. 'Whatever you do, do it unto the Lord!' " I had never heard that principle before, and I went straight to my Bible to check it out. That morning I began to understand that there is no separation of the sacred and the secular for a follower of Christ. I decided to enjoy caring for my daughter and cleaning out the cabinet (there's a real miracle for you) rather than feeling sorry for myself. I did it as "unto the Lord."

Frances taught through the book of Ephesians one of those winters we lived in Ada. We studied the doctrinal truths in Ephesians 1 through 4, referencing Scriptures and seeking to understand the spiritual principles that Paul taught. As we worked through chapter 5, we came to the passage on marriage (vv. 22–33). At that point Frances announced that we would be studying these verses the next week. You should know that she was a feisty redhead with flashing brown eyes, an impish smile, and a vivacious personality. She told us in no uncertain terms that there were times you had to tell your husband "what's what," and that's just the way it was. But we didn't get to that lesson the next week.

We had an unusually cold winter that year in Ada, and for six weeks in a row we had an ice storm on Tuesday. JOY Bible Study and most Wednesday night church services were cancelled those weeks due to impassable roads and thick coatings of ice. The phone lines were the only things hot in Ada those six weeks. Everyone, especially the moms of young children, was going stir-crazy. When we finally met again, we were expecting the fiery Frances to teach us how to straighten our husbands out—we had a big crowd for that session. But as she opened her Bible, we were stunned to hear her say, "Girls, I have been wrong. These six weeks the Holy Spirit has severely dealt with me, and I am going to teach you something entirely different than I would have six weeks ago." Quietly she began to quote Philippians 2:3, "Let nothing be done through selfish ambition or conceit, but in lowliness of mind let each esteem others better than himself." She then moved right into quoting Ephesians 5:22–24. You could have heard the proverbial pin drop. We didn't move. We hung on every word she said and instinctively knew that she was right.

True to form, Frances had studied this passage diligently and had wrestled with the text, which clearly linked Christ and the church with the dynamics of Christian marriage. As I recall, we stayed in that passage for a few weeks, until Frances was sure that we understood the principles. I must add that we agreed to forgive her for causing God to send ice storms to Ada, Oklahoma, six weeks in a row until she got it right. I have often thought of Frances's influence, her life example, and the richness of her teaching as being foundational to my philosophy of ministry. Frances died in 1996 from cancer, and I miss her to this very day.

It was watching Frances every Wednesday morning that whetted my appetite for teaching. I noticed the ease with which she handled Scripture and her wisdom in relating applicable truth to a group of women. I was stirred to begin more personal Bible study and devotional times, as well as taking opportunities to teach.

We were privileged to get to know Grace Chavis when we moved to Fort Lauderdale, Florida, in 1978. Grace taught a large young women's Bible study at our church, First Baptist, with an emphasis on marriage. Grace had a good command of Scripture, was an excellent communicator, and was culturally savvy as well. She understood the implications of feminism (which was in full swing at that time) for Christian women and its destructive influence on the biblical model of marriage. Her class was promoted as a Bible study on marriage, which obviously appealed to the several hundred women that attended every Thursday.

Grace taught us the basic principles of marriage, along with studies on the Sermon on the Mount and the life of Jesus. She was a leader in our intercessory prayer ministry, praying and counseling hundreds of women through marital difficulties. But the thing that made Grace's teaching so powerful was her own example. She was married to a man who was not a Christian, was not a member of the church, and claimed that he never would be. In fact, he was quite outspoken about his unbelief. According to Grace's testimony, as a young woman she directed the Servicemen's Center in Fort Lauderdale, where she met a charming naval officer named Colie Chavis. He swept her off her feet and she married him, despite knowing in her heart that she would be "unequally yoked" (2 Corinthians 6:14).

Grace had inherited a wonderful Christian heritage from her parents, but the year she met and married Colie was the one year she had decided to live life on her own terms. They went through several intense marital crises, and Grace desperately sought the Lord, that He might show her how to redeem this situation. Through her tears, intense prayer, and clinging to Scripture, Grace successfully learned how to apply biblical truths and principles to her marriage relationship, despite being married to an unbeliever.

She would weekly remind the women in our study that the spiritual condition of their husbands was not their concern, it was God's. The wife's biblical mandate was to love her husband and respect him, honoring him as the head of their home. Grace would admonish the women not to preach to their husbands or annoy them with spiritual talk, and to *never* "accidentally" leave tracts in the bathroom. She reminded us that God was more than capable of handling the spiritual condition of our husbands; our job was to pray for them, honor them, and live out our faith in a winsome manner.[7] She once told us that despite Colie not being a Christian, she always discussed with him any opportunities she had for speaking or serving in the church, and she would only do it if Colie was agreeable. She believed that even though Colie was not a Christian, God would give her direction through her husband. Who could argue with Grace? She lived those truths day in and day out for the last twenty years of their marriage. The principles she taught were applicable to anyone, married to a Christian or not.

Colie was retired by the time we moved to Fort Lauderdale, and he spent time tending to his orange trees. Therefore he was around the house and answered the phone frequently when any of Grace's young women friends would call. He would answer and loudly bark, "Chavis, here!" This usually terrified the woman on the other end (which he thoroughly enjoyed). Grace and Colie had a good marriage despite their differences, and my husband, O. S., had the honor of leading Colie to Christ before he died. I really cannot even estimate Grace's impact on the women of our church and community to this very day. Her willingness to not only teach sound doctrine but to flesh it out for us every day of her life made her an unforgettable example. I always enjoyed using Hebrews 13:9 whenever introducing or honoring Grace in some way because it is so true, "For it is good for the heart to be strengthened by grace" (NASB).

Grace eventually had to retire from teaching her class, due to caring for her elderly parents. She graciously asked me to begin teaching in her place, which was extremely courageous of her! With the encouragement of my husband and the prayers of many, I began to teach weekly. Those sessions were truly my "training ground" for speaking publicly, and I will forever be indebted to Grace for her confidence in me and for her pattern of good works. I must add that I also greatly appreciate the women who came every week and patiently listened to me. I know that they were not coming to hear me, but rather to hear from God, and I was always very aware of that fact.

*I*NTENTIONALLY developing relationships with younger women and looking for opportunities to connect with them on some level needs to be a priority.

The influence of these women and others has been woven into the fabric of my life, and their examples still motivate me to be more than I am. As I have been blessed in the past, I still benefit today from the faithful prayer ministry of Mary Jane Jennings, an older woman who has been my dear friend for the last several years. When I need prayer, the first person I call is Mary Jane. These connections with women who are further along the path of life than I am has always been a safe place for me, and I am forever grateful for them. Every year when I read the August 31 devotional in *My Utmost for His Highest,* I thank God for them and pray that I may be the same for others. "A person who has the right relationship with God lives a life as natural as breathing where he goes. The lives that have been the greatest blessing to you are the lives of those people who themselves were unaware of having been a blessing."[8]

## Teaching by Word and Example

As I look back at my life and what these women brought to me, I am reminded that I need to look forward as well. Intentionally developing relationships with younger women and looking for opportunities to connect with them on some level needs to be a priority. I don't necessarily think this influence must be in a formal mentoring setting, although I think those types of programs are an excellent idea. Forming intergenerational friendships and just being together, talking about the things women talk about, is beneficial to women of any age, and it's really enjoyable!

I have always noticed that usually the one place people of all ages and backgrounds connect is in the music ministry. Their mutual gifts and interests are an excellent setting for developing relationships despite age differences. Promoting healthy friendships between women of all ages strengthens the social fabric of the church, and it points toward honoring the Titus 2 principle.

If you are blessed to be at a church with a staff, meeting with the other ministers' wives is a great opportunity to build friendships, especially if it involves younger women. Despite any age differences, most staff wives welcome quality time together to pray, talk, and share together. During our years in Fort Lauderdale, I was blessed to have staff wives who understood how important this was. My dear friends Celia Reeder and Charlotte Hamilton were invaluable in this area, planning our staff wives' luncheons and always keeping this a priority in our busy lives. The opportunities to really visit with one another and to pray together would never have presented themselves in any other setting. I have also found that women who are on staff—not only the wives of staff members—enjoy these occasions also. They always have an added perspective on the life and ministry of a church. The one "rule" we had was this: what happens at the office stays at the office. We did not discuss any business between our husbands, church policies, or certainly any disagreements between staff members. That is nonproductive, to put it mildly, and takes the conversation places it should never go.

My friend Jeana Floyd, wife of pastor Ronnie Floyd, leads her staff wives with such excellence. She is a prime example of taking the directive of Titus 2 and deliberately working to build relationships and model Christian womanhood for the staff wives in her church. Every month she and the staff wives have lunch together and use the time to build relationships and converse about topics that specifically relate to them. Jeana's influence over the years has provided a model for many women who yearn for someone to show them how to live the "ministry life." She and Ronnie genuinely shepherd the staff couples and their families. Our mutual friend Kathy Ferguson serves on staff with the Floyds. As a former pastor's wife, Kathy has a unique perspective on Jeana's interaction with the other ministry wives in their church. She comments:

> Jeana generously and faithfully pours into the women who serve alongside their husbands on our staff. Staff wives are recipients of her care, her spiritual leadership, her training and teaching, and most importantly her friendship. Even after thirty years in ministry she willingly leads and loves young staff wives. She has tirelessly initiated a monthly ministry and sustained it for decades in order to invest in and encourage the ministries and staff marriages of a large multisite church. Most never see the quiet but powerful effect of her life on ministry wives.

Mary Somerville, author of *One with a Shepherd*, encourages this kind of investment in the lives of other women.

> If you are a senior pastor's wife, you can be investing in the other pastors' or elders' wives. If you are a young woman, you can mentor the leading girls in the youth group. Look for those women in your church with the bright eyes full of questions. Look for the ones who are eager to serve. Look for the ones who are faithful in the little things. Make time for them and your time will not be wasted. Have we caught hold of Paul's principle set forth in his letter to Timothy? He said, "And the things which you have heard from me in the presence of many witnesses, these entrust to faithful men,9 who will be able to teach others also" (2 Timothy 2:2, NASB).[10]

## Ministering to the Bereaved

There is probably no better opportunity for true ministry than comforting those who sorrow. Galatians 6:2 says, "Bear one another's burdens, and so fulfill the law of Christ." I regret that during our years in the pastorate, I did not make more of a deliberate effort to reach out to those who were grieving. Having gone through the grief of losing my vibrant sixty-four-year-old father, as well as other losses, I realize now how much an expression of love and compassion means.

I do think that there is something in our happy Americanized brand of Christianity that makes us turn away from suffering people. After all, as one woman told me, "It's just all so depressing." Yes, it is depressing to join others in their suffering, yet I think we are never more like Jesus than when we reach out to the hurting. The willingness to feel others' sorrow and enter into their suffering is a large part of what it means to bear one another's burdens.

A number of years ago I became friends with Verdell Davis Krisher, whose husband, Creath Davis, was killed in a plane crash in 1987, ending a marriage of almost thirty years. Verdell is a deep thinker and a writer, and I have been incredibly enriched by her friendship.[11] Listening to her share her journey over the years has added a rich dimension to my life and has encouraged me to reach out to others who are struggling with losses. Knowing the path Verdell walked as a young widow gave me another perspective on life and her walk with Christ has greatly enriched my life.

A few years ago our grandson, who was three years old at the time, had a serious eye injury while staying with us. It was a freak accident, but that was no comfort to my husband and me, since we were caring for him and his younger sister while our daughter and her husband were on a short trip. In those difficult days following his surgery and hospitalization, my husband and I clung to Scripture and words of comfort from our friends and especially fellow grandparents. My friend Teresa would frequently email me her prayers for us. Usually there was nothing in the email but her prayer, bringing our family to the throne of God, praying for our strength and asking for God's miraculous power to be demonstrated in Jackson's little eye. I printed her messages off and read them over and over, reminding myself of the truths that I knew in my heart, but which felt so distant. Due to her example, I found that just praying for someone over email, simply writing the words with nothing else, is a good thing to do, especially if you don't know what to say. And let me add that *any expression of comfort is better than none.*

I also suggest that you offer your own condolences, especially if you know the person who is grieving. I have not always done this, but I should have. Don't let your husband's participation in funeral services or expressions of sympathy be a substitute for yours.

Henri Nouwen, a writer who never fails to bring me fresh insight, sums it up in these words:

We say, "Why should I visit this person? I can't do anything anyway. I don't even have anything to say. Of what use can I be?"

Meanwhile, we have forgotten that it is often in "useless," unpretentious, humble presence to each other that we feel consolation and comfort. Simply being with someone is difficult because it asks of us that we share in the other's vulnerability, enter with him or her into the experience of weakness and powerlessness, become part of uncertainty, and give up control and self-determination. And still, whenever this happens, new strength and new hope is being born. Those who offer us comfort and consolation by being and staying with us in moments of illness, mental anguish, or spiritual darkness often grow as close to us as those with whom we have biological ties. They show their solidarity with us by willingly entering the dark, uncharted spaces of our lives. For this reason, they are the ones who bring new hope and help us discover new directions.[12]

The church connection is a very significant part of our lives as ministry wives. It is through our communities that we live and work out our faith. It is through our relationships within those communities that we teach and lead other women to find clarity in their commitment to Christ, to their husbands and children, and to ministry.

*Reflection*

RECENTLY A NATIONALLY known pastor was forced to resign from his church due to a sexual scandal. It was, of course, on the front page of every major newspaper in the country. But the interesting thing about this scandal was the reaction of the pastor's wife. She wrote a letter to the women of the church that was circulated on the Internet and made available to the public.[13] In this letter she addressed the questions that she instinctively knew the women in her church were asking each other. She said that she had promised God at her wedding altar to love her husband for better or for worse, and that is what she intended to do. Her greatest desire was to keep her family together, restore the marriage, and to rebuild their Christian witness. As she closed, she asked the women to pray for her as she began to undertake the test of her lifetime.

I was amazed at the courage and leadership this displayed. She clearly understood that not only did the women in her church want to know how she was going to handle this situation, but they also needed to see her react in a spiritually mature way. Her response to this dreadful situation would no doubt be a pattern for other women who faced such heartbreak. As I read and reread that letter I asked myself, "Would I have the courage to write such a letter? Would I have enough sensitivity to realize that women were watching me closely, looking for my response? Could I find the spiritual strength to move out of my own pain in order to model a Christlike response for the women around me?" These questions lead us to consider how we see ourselves as models—or patterns—for the women in our churches or ministries. This woman's courage in addressing the women in her church indicates her true understanding of leadership.

# 6

# The Personal Connection:
## *Your Walk with God*

The most important connection of all is your individual connection or relationship with God. Being "in the ministry" certainly does not automatically guarantee close fellowship with Him, as we all know. We must intentionally find the time and energy to strengthen this connection, recognizing that we are each responsible for our own walk with Christ. When we finally stand at the judgment, we will not be able to say, "I'm with him!" and point to our husband. We are each accountable to pursue God's plan for our lives and to minister according to the gifts and opportunities He gives us.

## Your Spiritual Journey

This ministry is sustained by our spiritual lives, often described as a journey. The image of journey is woven throughout the biblical narrative. Abraham leaving Ur, Moses leading the Israelites out of Egypt and through the wilderness, the exiles from Jerusalem traveling to faraway Babylon—these are just a few examples of well-known journeys in the Old Testament. This image is expanded in metaphorical references, particularly in the Psalms. Alister McGrath, in his excellent book *The Journey*, puts it so well: "Thinking of the Christian life as a journey through the world offers us a vivid and helpful way of visualizing the life of faith."[1] McGrath then makes two points that support his statement. First, he says, "The image of a journey reminds us that we are going somewhere."[2] Our final stop will be the New Jerusalem, and this gives us a sense of joyful anticipation as we make this journey.[3] Secondly, we should note that making this journey does more than just take us to heaven. It is the process by which we grow and mature, as we continue to "press on to our goal."[4]

This is hardly a new insight. John Bunyan wrote his classic, *The Pilgrim's Progress*, in 1678 and 1684 as an allegory on this spiritual journey, as did Hannah Hurnard in *Hinds' Feet in High Places*. These works involve imagination (typical of an allegory) and vividly illustrate the spiritual highs, lows, and challenges of the Christian's short time on this earth through story. Many other writers have used the figurative language of hills, valleys, and plateaus to describe the walk of faith.

As we each consider our own spiritual journey, it is helpful to see the larger picture. God has ordained the beginning and the end of our physical days here on this earth. Psalm 139:16 says, "In Your book they all were written, the days fashioned for me, when as yet there were none of them." Just as our physical birth was ordained by God, so was our spiritual birth. In the mysteries of God's will, we were chosen to make this journey, and it is God who set us on our path. "He chose us in Him before the foundation of the world, that we should be holy and without blame before Him in love" (Ephesians 1:4). Jesus says in John 15:16, "You did not choose Me, but I chose you and appointed you that you should go and bear fruit." Our spiritual life was initiated by God, and our assignment is to follow Him along this journey, wherever He leads, and with all of our heart.

All believers have markers along the road of faith. These are perhaps spiritual victories or insights, commitments, or events that solidify faith. But markers can also be times of struggle, and they are particularly helpful in understanding spiritual truth in hindsight—which, as they say, is twenty-twenty. One of my most loved and respected friends served on the mission field in a very difficult place for fourteen years and has as good a grasp on spiritual truth as anyone I have ever known. Several years ago, however, she went through a valley of doubt. For some reason, she began to question the truth of God's existence, His Word, His promises, and everything else that involves. Having been taught Scripture from childhood and being a mature Christian, this sudden crisis of faith was unnerving, and she couldn't understand it. I watched her wrestle with this challenge and listened to her talk through her emotions and questions. I listened to her, prayed with her, and am happy to report that she emerged from that spiritual battle stronger than she had ever been. That was a marker for her—a time of great struggle, but eventual victory. Markers serve us in the sense of staking out times of our lives that have spiritual significance and teach about this walk of faith. They also remind us that we are not meant to be permanent settlers in this world, but are simply passing through it temporarily.

My own spiritual journey started as a ten-year-old girl in Austin, Texas. My parents were faithful members of Hyde Park Baptist Church, and our pastor Ralph Smith led me to Christ and baptized me. I have never doubted that experience and can remember details of that day, even decades later. Even though I was active in church during most of my teen years, it took me awhile to figure out what the Christian life was all about. It probably was not until I was a young adult that I began to comprehend that my salvation experience was just the beginning of my walk with God.

One of the markers in my journey was our first trip to Israel in 1977. It wasn't just the excitement of my first overseas trip that was significant or even being in the land of the Bible. It was a worship service that our group attended at one of our Baptist missions, led by our missionaries there in Israel. The worship time at the service consisted of singing "Scripture songs,"[5] something with which I was totally unfamiliar. The soaring melodies, beautiful harmonies, and biblical language just overwhelmed me. I had never experienced a worship service in that way; it was so touching and emotional. My husband and the other friends we were with quickly began to learn the songs, eager to take them back to our church family in Oklahoma. That began a love for Scripture songs in my own life that has never left me. I am also a great fan of hymns and many praise songs, but nothing touches the depths of my heart as Scripture songs do. Even to this day, when I am discouraged or weary, those songs minister to my heart and strengthen me in the Lord. The only way I know how to describe how that music affects me is to say that it "restores my soul." As I think back on that experience, I am also reminded that often markers come along when you least expect them.

Like all followers of Christ, I have been on the "mountaintop" due to answered prayer or dramatic spiritual experiences as I just described. I have also been in valleys because of disappointment, loss, or hurt. And I have often been on plateaus—long and winding roads that sometimes seem to be going nowhere. Those plateaus are the dry times, when I feel spiritually weak or scattered, sometimes just going through the motions of being a Christian. However, keeping this image of a journey in my mind has helped me through those days, and it encourages me to continue pushing on as I realize that despite the winding road, I am definitely headed to a specific destination!

One of my favorite passages of Scripture is Psalm 84, particularly verse 5: "Blessed is the man whose strength is in You, whose heart is set on pilgrimage." Every time I read this verse, I am reminded that I have purposely set my heart on making this journey. The following verses hold out the promise of blessing for those who travel that way: "As they pass through the Valley of Baca [lit. *weeping*], they make it a spring; the rain also covers it with pools [or *blessings*]. They go from strength to strength; each one appears before God in Zion" (Psalm 84:6–7). The road occasionally leads through valleys of difficulty and sorrow, yet God's blessings enable the traveler to press on with strength and confidence. Alister McGrath says it this way:

> The journey we are invited to undertake is a long haul and delivers its benefits in the longer term. We have got to learn the hardest of all lessons—that we need to be patient. God seems to operate on a time scale that takes no account of our personal agendas and deadlines. The reality of life is such that we have to adapt ourselves to God's way of doing things rather than expect him to adapt to ours.[6]

This, then, is the essence of the journey. God has laid out the road for us and didn't even ask our opinion! He knows every twist and turn, every hill and valley, and He has promised to lead us as we follow Him in obedience and faith.

## Strength for Your Journey

It is ironic that for most of us, that ministry work usually competes time-wise with our own personal relationship with Christ. Yet we must guard that relationship above anything else. It is from that connection we find the energy and strength to fulfill our assignments. Oswald Chambers puts it this way:

> The most important aspect of Christianity is not the work we do, but the relationship we maintain and the surrounding influence and qualities produced by that relationship. That is all God asks

us to give our attention to, and it is the one thing that is continually under attack.[6]

It has been said that most of true ministry usually takes place in our lives as part of the "overflow" of our relationship with God. I believe that is true. Good Bible studies, conferences, or things of that sort are not the only things that demonstrate authentic ministry. It usually takes place in relationships—such as a spontaneous conversation or prayer with another person. This is the "overflow," the reservoir of spiritual understanding and truth that is filled in our daily walk with Christ.

> *I*T HAS BEEN SAID that most of true ministry usually takes place in our lives as part of the "overflow" of our relationship with God. I believe that is true.

Our daily quiet time of prayer and Bible reading feeds our spirits and gives us sensitivity to the Holy Spirit. During one of my particularly dry "plateaus" along my own spiritual journey, I realized that the reason I didn't feel like praying or reading my Bible was that I hadn't prayed or read my Bible! Physical hunger differs from spiritual hunger in that when one is physically hungry, she eats and is filled. But spiritual hunger is different. When you eat spiritual food you are satisfied, yet desire more and more. The way to stimulate our spiritual appetites is to simply fill our mind and hearts with the things of God. Jesus said, "Blessed are those who hunger and thirst for righteousness, for they shall be filled" (Matthew 5:6).

Someone once said, "You have all of God that you want." Our pursuit of God determines our spiritual depth. There was a time in my life when I felt God specifically calling me to a new dimension in my spiritual journey (one of my markers). I happened to be reading through Bruce Wilkinson's book *Secrets of the Vine* at the time. That little book helped me understand that God was inviting me to a closer walk with Him. The psalmist explains it this way: "When You said, 'Seek My face,' my heart said to You, 'Your face, Lord, I will seek'" (Psalm 27:8).

One of the things Wilkinson says is that our devotional time must broaden "from a morning appointment to an all-day attentiveness to His presence."[8] While I am sure most of us are aware on some level of God's presence all day, I like his verbiage of "all-day attentiveness." There is something so intentional about that phrase and it has stayed with me since that time.

I have also found that other spiritual disciplines besides prayer and Bible study are immensely helpful in strengthening my connection with God. A few years ago I felt impressed to begin to observe Lent, the six-week period that precedes Easter. While this is not a normal observance for evangelicals and was certainly new to me, I was surprised to find such satisfaction and blessing during those weeks. Traditionally the Roman Catholic and Orthodox churches have observed Lent through fasting, intense prayer, and repentance. From my understanding, however, this discipline can at times become legalistic or observed in some way that is not necessarily biblical. The true purpose of Lent is to set aside time for self-examination of sin, resulting in a fresh desire to follow Jesus. Since I haven't had great success fasting in the past, I let that go and decided to concentrate on repentance and prayer. I have other spiritual sisters who now walk this part of the journey with me (including my daughters), and we encourage one another along the way. There are some wonderful devotional books that keep me on track and focused on the sacrificial death of Christ and His resurrection. I begin to anticipate this observance after Christmas and to pray about what I should sacrifice during the coming season.

A few years ago I received a general email about fasting from bitterness, criticism, and other similar vices. I decided that season to fast from criticism, which turned out to be a dreadful revelation of how critical I actually found myself to be. I prefer to think of myself as being discerning, when in fact I discovered I was often cheerfully critical. That was one fast I wanted to be over; it was difficult. However, if I had not done it, I would never have seen the truth about myself in that area. I do think there is something significant about denying yourself something you enjoy or indulge in when observing Lent or on a spiritual fast. This perspective reminds us that we are on a journey. I also think it is another way of entering the story of the last weeks of Christ's life on this earth. Henri Nouwen says that observing Lent should never lead us to self-preoccupation, but to specifically "direct our attention to our loving Lord."[9] One of my friends spends an extra ten minutes in her quiet time reading through the Gospels during her Lenten observance. I can promise you this—once you observe Lent, Easter is never the same.

Please understand that I am not suggesting that everyone should observe Lent. I hope that I am simply illustrating that as we make this journey, we each need to make more than a halfhearted effort to cultivate our relationship with Christ. It is our spiritual life and health that enables us to receive the ministry and life work with which God has entrusted us. "My soul follows close behind You; Your right hand upholds me" (Psalm 63:8).

## Working Out Your Salvation in Service

In Philippians 2:12–13, Paul says to "work out your own salvation with fear and trembling; for it is God who works in you both to will and to do for His good pleasure." Clearly this does not mean that our salvation is a result of our works, but rather that God is working in us for our spiritual growth and sanctification. If someone said to you, "Work out your relationship with your husband," you would understand that meant to give time and attention to your marriage.[10] This is the very point Paul is making, urging the Philippians to give high priority to spiritual service and growth. "Working out your salvation" is not intended to gain God's favor or gift of salvation; it is the spiritual obedience of one who knows she is redeemed and desires to live according to God's purposes.[11]

But let's move from the theoretical realm to the practical. How do you "work out" your salvation as far as serving God? And how does this relate to the spiritual journey?

One of the most helpful things to do in discovering how to most effectively serve the Lord is learning to identify your spiritual gifts. Ephesians 4:12 says that God gives spiritual gifts "for the equipping of the saints for the work of ministry, for the edifying of the body of Christ." Christians using their spiritual gifts for the work of the ministry and for the building up of other believers is how God has chosen to operate in this world. Finding your gifts and using them appropriately not only strengthens the church, but also is personally fulfilling.

I can't even remember how many church responsibilities I accepted in the past just because somebody needed to do them. What I do remember is how bad I was at many of them. After eventually studying the passages on spiritual gifts and taking the obligatory tests, I discovered the most wonderful thing—usually your spiritual gift was something you truly enjoyed! This was the best news to me, and it makes perfect sense. For example, I found that one of my gifts was teaching. That was really no surprise, in the sense that I had always been drawn to that particular role. Nevertheless, I soon realized I had to develop that gift and learn study skills, how to dig into Scripture and think through logical outlines and thoughts. I am still working at those skills today. My point is this: learning how to use your gifts effectively and appropriately only increases your influence and contributions to the body of Christ.

Of course, taking on responsibilities in ministry is usually governed by your season of life, which also must be considered. If you have young children, you will have limited time for ministry responsibilities. In that case, I have always encouraged younger women to find what they really love (which usually relates to their spiritual gifts in some way) and do that one thing well. But your season of life may not be related only to age, but also to your husband's particular job. If he is a pastor, of course you will be primarily involved in your church. If he serves as a seminary or college professor, you automatically have opportunities with the student body. If you are in parachurch ministry, there will be specific opportunities offered accordingly. Finding what you love to do and then serving in a place that fits within your ministry calling develops your own walk with Christ.

There are also opportunities that come along that allow you to stretch yourself and do something that is not necessarily within your comfort zone. During our time in Fort Lauderdale, I was offered the opportunity to host a radio talk show at a Christian radio station in Miami, Florida. I had never done radio before and sought counsel from several trusted sources before I agreed to take this new responsibility. I distinctly remember the first night in the studio. While doing a sound check, I turned my head and caught a glimpse of myself with my headphones on in the reflection of the window that separated me from the sound booth. I had an instant rush of panic and thought, "What in the world am I doing? I have no idea how to do a radio show, and I start in three minutes!" By then it was too late to have second thoughts, and as we went on the air, I thought, "Well, when have I ever known what I am doing?" Hosting *Around the Table* gave me opportunities to think on my feet, and I discovered that I really enjoyed the edge of that kind of exchange. I also met many interesting authors and people whom I would never have talked with, much less interviewed. WMCU of Miami gave me the chance to stretch myself, and I will always appreciate it.

In 1997, my husband resigned the pastorate of First Baptist, Dallas, in order to accept the invitation to become president of Guide-Stone Financial Resources of the Southern Baptist Convention (formerly The Annuity Board). This agency oversees the benefits, insurance, and retirement funds of those working with Southern Baptist institutions, such as schools, churches, hospitals, and other evangelical ministries. This changed my life considerably, since we had served in the pastorate most of our married life. I will admit that it was a transition that at times was difficult for me. I enjoyed being a pastor's wife and loved the camaraderie of the church staff and connecting with the people in the church. But I also knew that since God had called us to this new work, He would have a new assignment for me. That is when the door opened for me to serve at Prestonwood Baptist Church in Dallas, Texas, as the director of women's ministry.

This was an opportunity to serve in an area I loved, but in a new capacity. My husband and I were attending church there, and it was a natural fit since we had been close friends with Jack and Deb Graham (the church's pastor and wife) for years. I found the women of Prestonwood strong, biblically literate, mission-minded, and eager to serve. I quickly realized that since I did not have the spiritual gift of administration (which I'm sure was very evident to everyone), that I would need to work extra hard in that area. I did not hesitate to lean on my ministry team to help me when I needed it, and they were always eager to do so. During those years, I learned something else—that administration is more important than I had ever realized. It's not just studying the budget or arranging tables and chairs in classrooms, things that seem "unspiritual." A structure needs to be created in order for women to use their gifts effectively. When spiritual gifts are utilized through thoughtful organization and are covered in prayer, real ministry takes place.

I am very grateful for that time at Prestonwood; it was invaluable to me. Serving on a church staff after being a pastor's wife for so many years was a new experience . . . and a good one! I will always be thankful for that time and especially for the lasting friendships that resulted from working and serving with the women there.

I am also grateful for the opportunity to develop administrative skills and to see firsthand how that gift enables the body of Christ to function smoothly. This was another marker in my spiritual journey—part of working out my salvation.

Every year in January, I ask the Lord to give me a verse for that year to pray through, something a prayer group in Fort Lauderdale taught me to do. It might be a virtue I need to work on, or a promise I need to claim, but it is always a Scripture I feel drawn to, not something I randomly choose. One year my verse was Psalm 43:3, "Oh, send out Your light and Your truth! Let them lead me; let them bring me to Your holy hill and to Your tabernacle." I would be turning fifty the next year, and I felt compelled to begin praying and thinking about the following years of my life in relation to my spiritual journey. What did I want to do with the years God was graciously giving me? How did I want to invest it in His work? I prayed that God's light and truth would lead me in this next stage and that I would be obedient.

I also sensed that John 15:5 should be my guiding verse for this next decade: "I am the vine, you are the branches. He who abides in Me, and I in him, bears much fruit; for without Me you can do nothing." I did not want more things to do; I had plenty to do. (Who doesn't?) I did not want to work harder, but I wanted to work wiser. I wanted to invest my time and energies in areas of life that would bear the most fruit for the kingdom of God. Around that time, I had begun to think about returning to school to work on a graduate degree. The Criswell College offered excellent theological education and was located in Dallas. After encouragement from friends my age who had already taken this plunge, I began my formal theological education. I must add that my husband was very supportive about my returning to school. I'm not sure if this was because he thought I really needed it, or if it was just a great way to keep me out of the mall, but his enthusiasm was a huge factor in my decision.

As anyone will tell you, when you return to school as an adult, it is quite different than during the college years. You actually want to learn, and there is not the usual pressure to get a degree as soon as possible, as is normally the case in young adulthood. I loved the classes, the discussions, my professors, and everything related to school. I discovered new topics of interest to me, such as women in church history. Even writing papers (which I initially dreaded) turned out to be spiritually beneficial. My theological education was one of the very best things I ever did, and if I had more years, I'd do every bit of it over again. More than once I would leave class and just sit in my car, reflecting on what I had learned, praying that I would remember it and use it in my daily walk. My prayer those years was that I would gain knowledge and insight, and that the offspring of that marriage would be an increased passion for serving Christ.

Not long after graduating, I was having my devotional time and came upon Psalm 43:3, the verse I had prayed through several years before. I suddenly realized how God had answered that very prayer. He had so clearly led me with His light and His truth, and they had brought me into a new and clearer understanding of His ways—His "holy hill." How faithful He is. This was another marker on my journey.

Working out our salvation will look different for each of us. Theological education, for example, strengthened my resolve at a particular point in my life. At other times, I have found fulfillment in working with young married couples, women, and children, or serving in other ways. Whatever we do, our goal should be the strengthening of our faith through our service. First Peter 4:10 says, "As each one has received a gift, minister it to one another, as good stewards of the manifold grace of God."

## Accepting Your Assignment

A large part of our spiritual journey has to do with accepting the assignment God has given us. At times we are in places (literally and figuratively) where the sun is shining and the road is smooth, where it is a pleasure to serve. Then there are the rough spots in our journeys, where serving is not so easy. Often we find a tension between our expectations and our assignments.

God calls us at times to hard places, to difficult ministries. As I write these words, I am thinking of several young families we met recently on a mission trip. These young couples are continuing their seminary educations through not only academic studies but also by living in countries that are closed to the gospel. They work at cultivating relationships with neighbors and believers (if there are any), learning the language, and praying for their people group. All of these couples have babies or young children, and we were amazed at their faith and spiritual strength. Nevertheless, these are hard places to serve, especially at that season of life. One of the young women told me, "You don't know how wonderful it is to hear English all the time! I didn't realize how hard I was working just to understand casual conversation." These are ministries that we expect to be difficult, but that doesn't necessarily make the journey any easier.

Then there are the long-term assignments that are especially challenging. Sometimes the places to which we are called are not particularly friendly to ministry families, and I don't mean in the sense of people being nice. Rather, these are places where churches perhaps are scarce, finances are limited, and people are unwilling to change or adjust to new ways of doing ministry.

One of my friends and her husband pastored churches in the Midwest for several years. She told me that most of the ministry wives she knew had to work full time due to financial pressures. (In fact, one statistic says that at least 70 percent of ministry wives work outside the home.[12]) Many of their husbands did not have benefits or retirement through their churches, so the wife's employment was a necessity. It would be a luxury for some pastors' wives to just concentrate on their spiritual growth and ministry to their women, but their circumstances don't allow it. The wife not working may be the ideal, but it is just not reality. According to my friend, these men are faithful pastors, but often their wives and children are frustrated by the pressures. Still, most of them "stay in those situations, doing the best they can out of a sense of calling."[13] I know these observations are not only true in the Midwest, but everywhere else as well. A former pastor who now works with smaller churches in the Southeast recently told me exactly the same thing.

This topic of ministry wives who work outside of the home needs more exploration. While most need employment for financial reasons, some wives feel that a vocation is part of their personal ministry. Sandee Hedger serves with her husband in a denominational capacity, working with ministry families. She recently made this observation to me:

Those called to serve within the borders of the United States would do well in applying the same missional approach to U.S. assignments demonstrated internationally by our missionary personnel. God calls us to a people group located within a specific situation (aka: local church). There are times when that calling includes an invitation to work outside the home, due to financial needs or the sense that God wants to use you outside the traditional setting of ministry life.

Our response should be: "If God has called us to serve here, and this is what it takes for us to serve here, then I embrace it as a part of the calling and will bring Him glory through this service." It is an "assignment" by God. By living the life of a Christ follower on the job site, we have the opportunity to demonstrate what a life touched by His grace looks like up close and personal with colleagues of various backgrounds and world views.

Rather than viewing employment as a burden, embrace it as a positive contribution to your witness. However, we must be especially mindful of maintaining the priority of our homes and families, especially when there are children still at home. This is our primary responsibility as wives and mothers. Many ministry wives find that working in the school system of their community, for example, provides them with the benefits they need and a schedule that works for their young families. Some work from home (thank you, Internet), while others are in the more traditional "nine-to-five" workforce. Whatever the situation, finding the balance of family, work, and ministry is very challenging. However, many ministry wives manage to do it with God's help. It is likely that in the future ministry wives will increasingly be in the workforce, meaning that we need to have a theological perspective as it relates to this topic.

## The End and the Beginning

Our journey is not complete until we finish our calling on Earth. The nature of our calling may change from time to time, but as long as we are alive and willing, we have purpose in our lives. I am frequently reminded of this due to my connection with GuideStone. One of the most enjoyable things I do is to direct our Widows Might Prayer Ministry.

We have almost a thousand widows in our prayer ministry—women who were married to pastors or missionaries and are now widowed, with an average age of over eighty. While the majority of them are in poor health, they nevertheless are quite eager to be involved in ministry through their prayer lives. I often describe them as weak in the flesh, but strong in spirit! Three times a year we collect prayer requests from our seminaries and other agencies. We send them in the form of a newsletter to our widows to inform them about what is happening in our churches and convention, and to ask for their prayers. Frequently we receive notes from them, saying how delighted they are to be included in this ministry and how seriously they take these prayer requests. One thing I have noticed: they all mention their husbands and how much they miss them. Almost every single woman says, "My husband was one of the best preachers in the whole country!" They always say how they appreciate being included in this prayer ministry and that they take this responsibility very seriously. Every time I read one of their letters, I pray that I will be as eager to serve the Lord at that stage of life as they are. While I will never see most of them face-to-face, we all share a sweet fellowship together due to our common prayers. They see this opportunity as part of their ministry as they are in the final stages of their journey. This is working out your salvation—finding a place to serve wherever you are, despite your age or physical limitations.

One of my favorite verses is Psalm 20:4, "May He grant you according to your heart's desire, and fulfill all your purpose." These widows who are praying faithfully for the work of the ministry are still fulfilling their purposes. As we make this journey with Christ, the desires of our heart are conformed to His, and He determines where to place us and how to use us in His kingdom work. What more can we ask?

Alister McGrath has a powerful perspective on the final part of our journey. He points out that every step along this road has been traveled by many others. We learn from those in the past and are comforted by those with whom we now travel. "And—finally!—we may rejoice in sure knowledge that one day we shall join them in the New Jerusalem, our journeying finally ended, as we raise our voices together in praise at the glorious sight of our Lord and Savior and eat and drink with Him in the kingdom of God. The journey will then have ended; something else more wonderful will have begun."[14]

*Reflection*

◆ Think over your own spiritual journey. Where did it begin? What are some of your markers? Think back over your own mountaintops, valleys, and plateaus. Where did you learn your most valuable lessons?

◆ What spiritual disciplines or experiences have significantly influenced your journey?

◆ What areas of service have you found the most fulfilling? What are some of the things you would love to do in the future? Begin to pray that all of your purposes will be fulfilled.

# PART 2
## *The Disconnects*

DISCONNECTION: to sever a connection;

dissociate; to terminate a connection; to become

detached or withdrawn[1]

# 7

# The Disconnect of Criticism:
## *Think What They Would Say if They Really Knew You!*

*"Criticism is something we can avoid easily by saying nothing, doing nothing, and being nothing."*[1]

—ARISTOTLE

One of the most challenging issues a ministry wife can face is the sting of criticism. It's hurtful when you are the one being criticized, and it's doubly hurtful when it is your husband who is criticized. But when it's your children—that is the worst of all. Disapproval is inevitable in ministry life, since it requires saying and doing a great deal. There are always ample opportunities for criticism.

My purpose in this chapter, however, is not to discuss criticism as simply something we should dismiss or always see as a negative of ministry life. A better approach is to understand how criticism—or negative judgment—should affect us and how to cope with it in a more positive way.

Criticism is usually viewed as coming from negative people

who enjoy doing the Devil's work. However, the Bible does not always support that view, since Scripture itself is filled with admonitions, instructions, and rebuke. Do a word study yourself, and you will find numerous verses that refer to the wisdom of being willing to receive instruction or correction. The book of Proverbs is full of verses that clearly indicate that it is a wise person who will heed a rebuke. Consider the following verses:

- "Do not correct a scoffer, lest he hate you; rebuke a wise man, and he will love you. Give instruction to a wise man, and he will be still wiser; teach a just man, and he will increase in learning" (Proverbs 9:8–9).
- "Whoever loves instruction hates knowledge, but he who hates correction is stupid" (Proverbs 12:1).
- "The ear that hears the rebukes of life will abide among the wise. He who disdains instruction despises his own soul, but he who heeds rebuke gets understanding" (Proverbs 15:31–32).
- "It is better to hear the rebuke of the wise than for a man to hear the song of fools" (Ecclesiastes 7:5).

Most of us are willing for God to rebuke us (or at least we say we are), but we are not so willing for other people to correct us. As we look at this topic, we will draw a contrast between two scenarios in Scripture where criticism was central: the stories of Nehemiah and King David. The book of Nehemiah tells the story of a Jewish man who returned to Jerusalem from the Babylonian exile in order to rebuild the city walls (approximately 445 BC). The city was in a hopeless state of disrepair, but Nehemiah provided the leadership and skill needed to lead the Jews in such an undertaking. It was a daunting project and took extensive organization and planning. As you might expect with such a venture, it didn't take long for him to become the object of bitter criticism. Those who governed there were not at all pleased with this return and plan for rebuilding. His enemies did everything they could to discourage and prevent Nehemiah from succeeding. However, they were not successful, and we will see how this remarkable man was able to withstand the criticism and accomplish God's work in Jerusalem.

The other story we will look at is the infamous account of King David and Bathsheba as told in 2 Samuel 11. David committed adultery with Bathsheba, the wife of Uriah, one of his military officers. After hearing that she was pregnant, David came up with a plan to hide his guilt. He deliberately sent Uriah into battle, placing him in a position where his death would be unavoidable. Uriah died in battle just as David had planned, and after Bathsheba had mourned for a period of time, David married her. Of course this whole incident was very displeasing to God.

Second Samuel chapter 12 begins with the prophet Nathan approaching David and confronting him with his sin. The significance of this hinges on the fact that Nathan was the king's trusted prophet, who regularly offered wise counsel, prayers, and spiritual support. So, naturally, the unpleasant task of rebuking the king fell to him. Nathan took an extraordinarily wise approach by relating a story, or word picture, that illustrated David's sin with Bathsheba and Uriah (2 Samuel 12:2–4). To David's credit, he instantly recognized himself in Nathan's parable and confessed, "I have sinned against the Lord" (2 Samuel 12:13).

These two stories contain distinct reactions to serious criticism. Some of us have walked in Nehemiah's shoes, knowing that we are being obedient to God's call, and we are able to disregard our critics. Others of us identify with David, who saw his own disobedience and error and responded in a biblical manner. In order to correctly assess criticism, we need to do three things: consider the source, check our motives, and then evaluate it correctly.

## Consider the Source

Bear in mind the one who has criticized you. Is this someone you respect? Or is it someone who is a chronic complainer? Is this someone who knows what they are talking about, or is it someone who is just being negative and judgmental?

In one of our former churches we had a man who was a very successful businessman and was generous with his tithes and offerings. He was quite proud of seeing his name on a plaque on the grand piano in the church auditorium (one of his gifts to the church), and he always pointed out his giving record to anyone who would listen. Just about every Monday morning, he would pull into the church parking lot and head straight for the office. The administrators would quickly spread the word, "He's here!" and instantly vanish from their desks if there was time. His purpose was to "help" them by pointing out every mistake in the church bulletin from the previous Sunday. He complained about everything—from the staff to the programming to the Sunday school organization. The interesting thing was that he actually had some good points and valid criticism. But who wanted to listen to him? He clearly had not learned that criticism is best taken when couched between praise and affirmation. The result was that no one paid attention to him or even remotely cared what he thought, no matter how many typos appeared in the bulletin. No matter how well things might have been done that Sunday, you could be sure he would find something to complain about.

Prior to our pastorate there, a revival service was given over to forgiveness and reconciliation among the church members. Not surprisingly, there was a line of people after the service at his pew, convicted of their negative feelings toward him. His comment? "It's about time these people apologized to me." What are you going to do with someone like that? Just consider the source and understand that there is truly no pleasing some people. And be extremely grateful you are not married to him!

In Nehemiah 2:10, we see one of the reasons Nehemiah was able to disregard the barrage of criticism directed at him. Sanballat and Tobiah, his political enemies, "were deeply disturbed that a man had come to seek the well-being of the Children of Israel."

They did not have the interests of the Jews at heart, but rather their concerns were for their own political power and prestige. They saw the return of the Jews and the rebuilding of the city walls as a threat to their own territory. In chapter 6 they conspired with some of their own enemies to destroy Nehemiah's work, a perfect illustration of the saying, "The enemy of my enemy is my friend." They invited Nehemiah to a "meeting" on the plain of Ono, but he was wise to their strategy and must have said, "Oh, no! No Ono!" After four efforts and Nehemiah's repeated rebuff, they finally came up with Plan B. According to Nehemiah 6:6–7, they sent him a letter which began by saying, "It is reported." (which can be interpreted, "They say . . .") that Nehemiah was planning a rebellion and rebuilding this wall so that he could be king. They claimed that Nehemiah had even appointed prophets to proclaim this as part of his plan. Nehemiah responded by saying how totally ridiculous the accusations were and that he would stay right where he was. By understanding that the source of criticism was from those who hated the Jews and had no regard for their well-being (spiritual or otherwise), Nehemiah could dismiss the criticism and concentrate on the work.

In contrast, look at the story of David and Nathan. Despite David's stunning disregard for God's law shown by adultery and murder, he instantly recognized himself in Nathan's parable. It needs to be noted here that David could easily have sent Nathan packing, since David was the king. There are no checks and balances in a monarchy! But David did respond, and we see his repentant heart in Psalm 51, which is one of the most poignant chapters in the Bible. He received Nathan's rebuke simply because he respected and trusted this prophet. David knew that Nathan most definitely had his best interests at heart and had even risked his own life in confronting this horrific sin.

I have also been the recipient of criticism, like everyone else. It is always a little easier to swallow and to manage when it is spoken with your well-being in mind, especially if it is from someone you respect. Considering the source is a wise thing to do when evaluating criticism.

## Check Your Motives

It is always wise to do some self-investigation when you are on the receiving end of criticism. Why did you do or say what you did? Were your motives and intentions pure?

Let's be very honest here: we all have an amazing capacity for self-justification. Unless you take time to really think and pray through criticism, your heart will always put your actions and motives in the best light. I know that I have relived times of being criticized in my own life over and over again until I am convinced that I am so innocent that I could actually be one step away from canonization as Saint Susie. I am reminded of something someone once said, "When you are criticized unjustly, just think what they would say if they knew the truth." That definitely puts criticism in the right perspective.

Nehemiah knew without a doubt that his plan and work was a mission from God. He says in chapter 2, verse 12, "I told no one what my God had put in my heart to do." This was an indication of Nehemiah's pure heart. He had not been plotting and planning or positioning himself for political power. Rather, he knew that from the very beginning of this endeavor, God had planted this desire within his heart. That was his only agenda.

David, on the other hand, quickly recognized his sin that resulted from his evil motives, which he had not admitted until Nathan's rebuke. Perhaps this is why he said in Psalm 51:6, "Behold, You desire truth in the inward parts, and in the hidden part You will make me to know wisdom." He then prayed in verse 10 for God to "create in me a clean heart," another confession of his sinful heart and actions.

There are times in all of our lives when our motives are not pure. I encourage all of us to relentlessly strive to see how deceitful our hearts can be. This may come through the gentle rebuke from a fellow believer, as it did for David, or it may be a result of self-examination. The prophet Jeremiah said, "Let us search out and examine our ways" (Lamentations 3:40). This takes work, and it's not very pleasant. Nevertheless, it is the only way that we can clearly identify where we need to accept correction. Augustine prayed, "O Lord, deliver me from this lust of always vindicating myself."[2] God said in Jeremiah 17:9–10, "The heart is deceitful above all things, and desperately wicked; who can know it? I, the Lord, search the heart, I test the mind, even to give every man according to his ways, according to the fruit of his doings." Only the Spirit can reveal the hidden parts of our heart and reveal them to us. In Psalm 19:14, David says, "Let the words of my mouth and the meditation of my heart be acceptable in Your sight, O Lord, my strength and my Redeemer." Our true motives are hidden in the meditations of our heart. It is not easy to face them, but if we are going to take a close look at the criticism we receive, we must follow David's lead.

## Evaluate the Criticism

To evaluate something means to examine it and judge it. This is what we need to do when we have been the target of criticism. If you have the presence of mind to do so, it is good to be certain that you heard the person's words right. Don't read more into criticism than was intended. Sometimes we exaggerate a small thing into something monumental that was never that important in the first place. I know that in the past when I have heard a critical comment about my husband, I have immediately started imagining how the entire church has never truly appreciated him, his preaching, or his leadership. Before I know it, I will have us marching to martyrdom due to our dreadful sufferings. When that happens, I know to step back and not allow my immediate defensiveness to determine how I respond. If someone criticizes something my husband does, I usually say, "You need to make an appointment and talk to him about that. Talk to me if your concern is with me or our kids." Usually they will not have the nerve to talk to him; it is much easier for them to say something critical to you, or worse, the children.

When someone criticizes our children, we need to evaluate the criticism privately in order to handle it wisely. I had a friend once who would occasionally say something to me that was "borderline" critical about one of my daughters in a half-joking manner. The first time it happened, I was so surprised that I wasn't sure I heard it right. The next time, however, I didn't respond at all (which was awkward, to say the least), hopefully sending her a message. From that point on I intentionally avoided any conversation about our children with her, which wasn't easy since we were friends. However, I do think she noticed, since the comments stopped. And, to be honest, I also watched my daughter a little more closely to see if there was any truth to the criticism. I do think ministry moms may need to give extra attention to this area and keep the lines of communication open in order to talk these things through with our children.

Ask yourself if there is any truth to the criticism. Is it simply exaggerated for the benefit of the one criticizing or is it legitimate? You may need to speak to someone whom you trust to help you think it through. Or perhaps you need to backtrack and clarify what was meant or said. As you do, you may be able to learn something from it that would benefit you in the future.

Evaluate the criticism in light of God's law. Is it a moral issue? Is it a theological issue? These are very important points and must be taken seriously. In Galatians 2, Paul issued a scalding public rebuke of Peter in front of other believers for his hypocrisy in associating with Jewish believers to the exclusion of the Gentile ones. While this may seem insignificant to us, it was extremely important at that time. The Judaizers (Jewish believers) were claiming that in order to be a Christian, one had to be circumcised and observe the Jewish law. This was a volatile issue that threatened the existence of the early church and had to be dealt with immediately. When Peter showed preference to the Judaizers at the meeting, he was giving credibility to their erroneous view. Yet Peter had a crystal clear understanding of the nature of salvation, and he knew that the teaching of the Judaizers was completely false.

In Paul's view, Peter was compromising truth in this situation and had to be corrected—the purity of the gospel message was at stake. We can safely say that Peter was never at his best when it came to peer pressure, and this was no exception. We have no record of his response to Paul's confrontation, but we do have his epistles, 1 and 2 Peter. These letters contain profound insights relating to the nature of the sacrificial death of Christ, in addition to passages on suffering and guarding against false teaching and practices. Peter surely understood that Paul's criticism was warranted because it was related to theological error, which had to be corrected for the good of the early church.

*THE ULTIMATE challenge in handling criticism is determining if it is irrelevant or if it is a warning or rebuke from God.*

Another example of criticism in Scripture is found in Numbers 12, where Aaron and Miriam (Moses' brother and sister) criticized Moses for marrying an Ethiopian woman. However, the reader knows that was a surface issue, since verse 2 reveals that they were really jealous of Moses since God only spoke through him. In this case God took care of the criticism Himself, calling Moses, Aaron, and Miriam to a meeting at the tabernacle. He "came down in the pillar of cloud and stood in the door of the tabernacle," and called Aaron and Miriam to come forward (Numbers 12:5). God then rebuked them for their criticism of Moses and defended him. In verses 6–8, God made it very clear that He chose to speak to Moses "face to face," not to Aaron and Miriam, and that He would continue to do so. As punishment for their criticism, Miriam was struck with leprosy. Aaron and Moses cried out to the Lord for mercy and begged for her healing, which He granted after seven days. In this case, Moses could dismiss the criticism, especially since God Himself handled it for him. However, in evaluating this situation, we can see that Aaron and Miriam did not have pure motives; they were just jealous of Moses. As far as his marriage, all one can conclude is that God didn't seem to object to Moses marrying this woman, since He never addressed it as far as we know. This criticism did not relate to a moral or theological issue, but was rather just another petty criticism of a leader.

## Take It or Leave It

The ultimate challenge in handling criticism is determining if it is irrelevant or if it is a warning or rebuke from God. He generally uses people to accomplish His purposes, so it could be from the Lord. Of course, God also uses His Word to rebuke and instruct, but if it comes from a person, it gets our attention and is usually harder to overlook than a verse of Scripture. But sometimes God uses circumstances to rebuke us and teach us a valuable lesson.

A number of years ago while we were still in the pastorate, I experienced this very thing. My husband and I were planning to attend a Sunday school leadership banquet one night at our church. Our speaker was a popular preacher from another part of the country, and he was arriving just an hour or so before the banquet began. Late that afternoon I was doing all those things moms do— arranging dinner for the kids, picking up the babysitter, and so on. I did not plan my time well and found that I only had a few minutes to dress before it was time to leave. As I rushed into the bedroom to dress, my husband held out the shirt he had planned to wear and casually asked me to sew on a button that was missing. My reaction was about as bad as it could be. I stared at him and said, "Are you kidding me? You have plenty of shirts; wear another one!" He immediately picked up on my exasperation (oh, he is a perceptive one) and agreed to do so. But no, that wasn't enough for me. I snatched the shirt, fussing and fuming, madly sewing on the tiny, ridiculously insignificant, and unnecessary button so the pastor would be well dressed for the Sunday school banquet. As I was doing this, I knew that I was being dreadfully disobedient. I knew better than to act the way I was, I knew that I should have been gracious and loving, but I didn't want to be. The disagreement escalated, and as we drove to the church there was very little conversation as I madly applied makeup and tried to do something with my hair.

When we arrived, we pulled the old familiar act of cheerfully greeting people while being very irritated with each other. (I am sure all of you have participated in this game occasionally.) The banquet began, and after we ate, our guest speaker stood to deliver his message on leadership. His first point was that our attitude toward serving others was an indication of our true commitment to Christ. I began to feel slightly uncomfortable when he mentioned attitude, but things quickly got worse. He then offered an illustration: "Let's say that O. S. needs Susie to sew a button on his shirt. Now let's just *imagine* that Susie gets angry and complains about this, revealing a bad attitude on her part." Of course everyone laughed and looked at me, since they simply couldn't imagine that a sweet, little pastor's wife would do such a thing. He went on to explain that true service in the kingdom of God is best demonstrated by a spirit of graciousness. Of course he was smiling and the audience was amused, having no idea that that exact thing had just happened and I was being seriously reprimanded. The speaker had no clue either as to what had happened that late afternoon, since he had arrived just before the banquet began. I glanced over at my husband, who, I might add, was enjoying this whole scenario entirely too much. I didn't hear much else the speaker said, because I was busy repenting and confessing my sin before it got worse!

As I considered the source of this rebuke, I knew that the speaker had no prior knowledge of my little fit and was innocently delivering his message on leadership. Judging my own motives didn't take long, since I was forced to admit to myself that my agitation was entirely my own fault. I had probably talked on the phone too long and not planned my time well. If I had allowed enough time to dress, I would have had the extra few minutes needed to sew on that ridiculously insignificant and unnecessary button. As far as evaluating this correction from the Lord, that didn't take long either. I knew in my heart that I was wrong from my very first reaction and had no excuse. So I sat there with a phony smile pasted on my face while doing some serious groveling before the Lord in my heart. Later, when we drove home, I apologized profusely to my husband, who was still thoroughly amused by the whole incident. I fully deserved that rebuke, and I have never forgotten it, especially when asked to sew on a button. And I've always wondered if my husband tipped off the speaker . . .

That brings to mind a statement I once heard somebody say, "Blessed are those who persecute you, for they may be right!" Being courageous enough to confront our own sinfulness and yet discerning enough to know when criticism is unwarranted is the key to receiving correction. Proverbs 9:9 says that when a wise person heeds rebuke she is wiser for it. May God give us the grace to do that very thing.

## Reflection

---

◆ Can you think of a time you were criticized and thought about it from the perspective described in this chapter? Is there anything useful you could still learn from it?

◆ If you know that criticism directed toward you is not important or is even insignificant, can you let it go? Why or why not?

◆ Can you honestly pray Psalm 141:5? "Let the righteous strike me; it shall be a kindness. And let him rebuke me; it shall be as excellent oil; let my head not refuse it."

# 8

## The Disconnect
## of Pleasing People:
## *"I'd Be Happy to Do It!"*

*"Being obsessed with what people think about me is the quickest way to forget what God thinks about me."*[1]

—CRAIG GROESCHEL

Everyone loved Terri.[2] An attractive young ministry wife who was eager to serve, Terri was unusually generous with her time and energy. She always managed to give extensive help to friends and acquaintances who asked for it, despite the stresses of her own job, church life, and family life. Anyone who needed an extra set of hands could depend on Terri to help, from church members to work colleagues to her extended family members. Everyone knew that she would never refuse their appeal. Terri was like an ATM machine—key in your request and out would come the help you needed. She prided herself on being a faithful friend, one who would never say no and was always available when needed.

Not surprisingly, Terri eventually found herself in a crisis where she was physically and emotionally exhausted. While in counseling (at the advice of another ministry wife), Terri learned something about herself: on the surface she appeared to be a "super saint," always sacrificing for others. However, Terri soon discovered that her motivation for doing so was really not so honorable. She was desperately seeking approval from people, rather than from God. Suffering from feelings of unworthiness and insecurity, Terri craved the respect and admiration of others. Complimentary words filled her "emotional tank" temporarily, but it never lasted. While she always received appreciation for her good deeds, she reluctantly admitted to her counselor that it was "never enough." One complaint or slight criticism would throw her into the depths of despair and begin the pleasing cycle all over again. Terri was an approval addict.

Terri, unfortunately, has a lot of company in the Christian community, especially with those in ministry. Whether many of us wish to admit it or not, our feelings of value are often based on our emotional state. We feel significant and loved as long as people like us and agree with us or support what we are doing. However, when criticism or rejection comes our way, we often follow in Terri's footsteps, believing that our perceived failures in the eyes of others simply prove our inherent unworthiness. Perhaps women are more prone to this tendency than men, due to our relational nature. While most men might shrug off a friend's disapproval, it is more likely that a woman will analyze it, brood over it, or confront it, in order to resolve the conflict.

It is essential that believers in Christ have a biblical understanding of approval. We all need and want the love, support, and respect of our church members, friends, and community. However, it is the mature Christian who will honestly examine her own heart and determine whose approval she is actually seeking—God's or man's. This is not an easy challenge, and it is helpful to have a listening ear to provide biblical guidance, balance, and wisdom. Pleasing others has its own rewards, but they are not lasting and certainly are not always in line with God's. The bottom line is that in seeking the praise of men, the focus is on me and not on God.

When God fashioned man, He designed him with an inherent need for relationships, such as marriage and family. In God's creation, this community was good. It is natural and healthy to want to belong to a group, living together and working in harmony. However, this desire is twisted when we become unusually afraid of disappointing people and are unable to balance or accept others' dissatisfaction with us. In ministry this is not unusual, simply because keeping other people happy is the best way to prevent complaining.

I have struggled with this myself. How many times have I walked away from a meeting thinking, "Why did I say I would do that? How can I get out of it?" This is because I tend to be a people pleaser myself. I like making things easier on people, and usually saying yes to some responsibility makes some people really happy. But this is not only unhealthy in the emotional sense, but also in the spiritual sense. The only approval we should be seeking is God's, since our purpose in this life is to accomplish the work He has given us.

In 2 Corinthians 5:9, the apostle Paul expressed a very important principle pertaining to this topic. "Therefore we make it our aim, whether present or absent, to be well pleasing to Him." The bulls-eye in the target of life for the Christian is the praise and approval of God, not man.

The context of the Scripture above is Paul's explanation of the judgment seat of Christ. Someday we will each appear before Him and give an account of our lives. Therefore, we must always remember that our highest calling is to please God, not others. With this concept firmly in mind, it is helpful to observe a few other points that reinforce this principle.

## Will You Still Love Me Tomorrow?

People are notoriously fickle and can change their minds or opinions in an instant. If we base our sense of worthiness on others' approval of us, we are going to be in trouble. The Bible is full of examples of the inconsistencies of human nature. Acts 14:8–20 records an incident that happened during the first missionary journey of Paul and Barnabas. While preaching in Lystra, Paul observed a lame man who "had faith to be healed." When the people saw this miracle, they began to shout, "The gods have come down to us in the likeness of men!" (v. 11). The priest of Zeus quickly brought oxen to the gates, in order to sacrifice them to their new gods, Paul and Barnabas. Paul and Barnabas were horrified and began to tear their clothes (a sign of distress), and cried out for the people to stop. They said, "We also are men with the same nature as you, and preach to you that you should turn from these useless things to the living God." (v. 15). The Bible records that despite all of their efforts, they "could scarcely restrain the multitudes from sacrificing to them" (v. 18).

> *I*T WOULD BE be beneficial for those of us in ministry to understand that the fickleness of human behavior will always be with us.

As if that wasn't enough commotion for one day, soon Jews arrived from Antioch and Iconium, who were enemies of Paul's. Verse 19 of chapter 14 says, "Having persuaded the multitudes, they stoned Paul and dragged him out of the city." Although the Bible says that they thought Paul was dead, amazingly he got up and left for Derbe the following day with Barnabas. Note the fickleness of this crowd—one minute they were literally worshipping Paul and Barnabas, preparing to sacrifice to them as if they were gods. A few hours later, after hearing from the Jews of Antioch, they proceeded to try to kill Paul. If Paul and Barnabas (and the early church, for that matter) had determined the success of their missionary journeys by the mood or acceptance of those who heard them preach, they would have been considered total failures. We know that we cannot judge the effectiveness of the gospel message simply by the surface or emotional reaction of people.

It would be beneficial for those of us in ministry to understand that the fickleness of human behavior will always be with us. This is true in the political world, the entertainment world, and the business world, not only in ministry. While it may be nice to enjoy high approval ratings for a while, it is inevitable that we will make decisions or do something that will cause those ratings to fall. That is simply a part of leadership. However, seeking God's favor or approval results in a sense of knowing we have honored Him and considered His approval rating of us.

## What Does Everybody Think?

It is also human nature to care about others' opinions more than God's. When we are rewarded with praise from people in the present, it is certainly more satisfying than waiting until we get our heavenly rewards! An example of this is found in John 12:42–43, "Nevertheless even among the rulers many believed in Him, but because of the Pharisees they did not confess Him, lest they should be put out of the synagogue; for they loved the praise of men more than the praise of God." These verses cut right to the quick and reveal the stark truth: men prefer praise from one another rather than from God. People will not do what their hearts may tell them to do, because of the fear of others' reaction or rejection. In this case, the Pharisees had the political clout to appoint leaders in the synagogue from the Jewish community. If one was "put out" of the synagogue, he no longer had any popularity, influence, or recognition (see also John 7:13).

Proverbs 29:25 says, "The fear of man brings a snare." Simon Peter fell into this trap as he sat outside the courtyard at the house of Caiaphas, the high priest (Matthew 26:69–75). Two servant girls and a small group of others recognized Peter as being one of the men who was with Jesus. Peter vehemently denied the truth, even cursing, as he declared, "I do not know the Man!" (v. 72). When the rooster crowed, Peter recalled Jesus' prophesy and "wept bitterly" (v. 75). How many millions of Christians have identified with Peter's experience? Even if we don't always deny Christ verbally, we often simply fail to speak a word for Him, which is just as bad. Afraid of the rejection of others, we silently let opportunities for a witness pass by. Philip Yancey, who is a very successful Christian author, wrote about this very thing once. He noticed his own reticence when given the opportunity to identify himself as a Christian to others while in a public setting such as an airport or on a bus. He asked himself some hard questions, such as "Why do I speak in generalities when strangers ask me what I do for a living and then try to pin down what kind of books I write? Why do I mention the secular schools I attended before the Christian ones?"[3]

It is our wretched human nature that causes us to desire man's approval rather than God's. In Peter's case, the opinion of a few people mattered more to him at the moment than the approval of Jesus. If we take more than a surface look at this incident, it becomes more significant. Peter had traveled with Jesus for three years, heard all His teachings, witnessed miraculous healings, and had numerous discussions with Him and the other disciples as they traveled or sat by the fire at night. He had a history with Jesus, and we know that despite Peter's failings throughout the gospel narrative, he loved Jesus with all his heart. This makes his denial of Christ even more disturbing. Yet if we are honest, we must confess that we sometimes do the same.

Of course, there is another view of this principle. As Christians, we know that we need to have good reputations in order to validate our witness. This doesn't mean that we totally disregard others' opinions or views of what we do. Especially being in leadership, we should listen to and consider the opinions of others.

However, our first and foremost goal must be obtaining God's approval, as opposed to the approval of others.

Paul succinctly puts it this way: "For do I now persuade men, or God? Or do I seek to please men? For if I still pleased men, I would not be a bondservant of Christ" (Galatians 1:10). If Paul had sought the praise of men, he would never have fulfilled the will of God for his life.

## Bad Decisions Bring Bad Consequences

Frequently I hear our daughters warning their children about the consequences of their occasional disobedience. In one instance, our daughter was disciplining our four-year-old granddaughter Halle for not sharing with one of her cousins. She firmly said, "Halle, that was a poor choice, and because of that you will have a consequence." As Halle was led out of the room, she looked back at me with her huge blue eyes framed by brown ringlets and said very sadly, "I'll be back after my consequence." It was hard not to smile, hearing the word "conthequenth" spoken by a four-year-old. But it was gratifying to know that she was learning this concept early. Bad decisions result in bad consequences for adults or children. Caring primarily about public opinion definitely affects one's ability to make wise decisions, and the Bible is full of examples that illustrate this truth. Consider each of the following.

### The Children of Israel

When the children of Israel were poised to enter Canaan, they were overcome with fear. They wept and complained to Moses and Aaron, even threatening to select a new leader and return to Egypt! Joshua and Caleb, two of the twelve spies sent to explore the territory, began to protest, saying that they had seen "exceedingly good land" (Numbers 14:7), and that if they obeyed the Lord, He would give it to them as He had promised. (Their report differed from the other ten spies, who strongly advised that they not attempt to enter the land.) Joshua and Caleb reminded the people that God was with them and there was no reason to fear the Canaanites. The Israelites' response was an attempt to stone Joshua and Caleb, whose death was prevented due to God's intervention.

The conversation between Moses and God that followed this event is really astonishing. God said that He was sick to death of His unbelieving people, and He was prepared to disinherit them. Moses pleaded with the Lord, saying that if He did such a thing, His reputation would be ruined with the Egyptians and the Canaanites. He begged God to forgive them, which God agreed to do. However, the ten spies who had given their negative report and advised the people of Israel against entering the Promised Land died in the wilderness as a consequence of their lack of faith. What if Moses, Joshua, and Caleb had listened to the will of the people? What if they had sought the people's approval of this plan rather than God's? They would have wandered in the wilderness for many more years and probably simply died out. However, Canaan was their destination, a vital part of God's plan for His people. In this case, the decisions of Moses and Joshua brought a welcome consequence—a rich and beautiful land that they would conquer and inhabit.

### King Herod

King Herod, who had a grudging respect for and fear of John the Baptist, made a decision he regretted when on an impulse he made a promise to the daughter of Herodias, his wife. At his birthday party, the girl performed a dance for him, and he was quite pleased. He promised "with an oath" to give her anything she asked (Matthew 14:7). We can only assume he thought she would ask for money or some material possession. Instead, having been well-coached by her mother, she asked for the head of John the Baptist. Herod regretted his promise, but because he didn't want to be embarrassed in front of his guests, he gave the command, and John the Baptist was killed (see Matthew 14:1–12).

## Pilate

Pilate, the governor of Judea, had the power to release Jesus or turn Him over to His accusers for crucifixion. After interrogating Jesus, Pilate announced to the crowd that he did not consider Jesus guilty of any crime that would require death. He even asked the crowd, "Why, what evil has He done?" (Mark 15:14). Pilate knew that the chief priests were turning Jesus over to him because of their envy of Him, not because He had broken any specific Jewish law. Yet because Pilate wanted "to gratify the crowd," he released the criminal Barabbas and turned Jesus over to be crucified (Mark 15:15). This proved to be a terrible decision with even worse consequences.

Looking for praise from people affects our ability to make a wise decision. A better place to start is on our knees, seeking God's wisdom and direction.

## Always Seeking, but Never Finding

When we live our lives seeking the approval and applause of others rather than God, we find ourselves in bondage. In one of our former churches I developed a friendship with a woman whom I will call Carol. We often had discussions regarding family, church, and all the other usual topics. One year before Thanksgiving we were in a group of women chatting about our plans. Carol began to share with us how much she dreaded the holiday because of her mother.

Being an only child, the holiday meal was always left to Carol, since her mother was elderly. While she didn't mind the cooking and enjoyed using her creativity (definitely one of her gifts) in preparing the dinner table, she dreaded hearing her mother criticize her efforts. She told us that throughout her entire life, nothing she did had ever been good enough for her mother. No matter what her age, her clothes were wrong, the purchase of a house was wrong, her job was wrong, the way she raised her son was wrong, her car was wrong—nothing she ever did resulted in affirmation from her mother. The amazing thing is that she was like a little girl, still craving her mother's approval, even though as an adult she knew she would never receive it.

Later on, privately, I probed a little further with Carol and asked her some questions. Her father had died at an early age, so there was not a dad to provide some kind of balance. The amazing thing was that she was still so desperate and intent on hearing her mother say, "I'm so proud of you! Well done!" Carol never received that affirmation and never stopped begging for it.

During our conversation I related an illustration I had just read somewhere on this very topic. If a well (a metaphor for parental approval) is always empty, why do you keep returning to it for water? You know that it will never give you what you so desperately want. When that happens, the real question is this: Who is the more emotionally sick person? Is it the one who cannot give approval or the one who continues to beg for it? Of course, neither person is emotionally healthy, but the one who continually begs for approval becomes just as dysfunctional as the one who can't give it. As spiritually mature adults, we must strive to "put away childish things" (1 Corinthians 13:11) and adjust our thinking to biblical patterns. Our ultimate approval is found in Christ, who loves us as we are. It is best to look at a person such as Carol's mom as simply emotionally disabled and unable to give the approval her child craves. Carol needed to accept her mom as she was and trust God to provide others in her life who could meet those emotional needs.

Not long after that conversation, her mother died and I spoke with Carol on the phone. I expressed my hope that she could find some peace of mind now in this area and not be so haunted by her mom's incessant disapproval. Her response was, "I would like to have peace of mind, but all I hear is my mother's voice telling me how I just never measured up." I recommended Christian counseling immediately. Carol's focus for most of her Christian life was not on finding God's approval, but searching for her mother's. Most of her energy in her adult life had been taken up with trying to please someone who could never give her what she wanted. How sad that we sometimes live in such bondage when freedom is available to us!

## Following Jesus, Our Example

As always, Jesus proves to be the perfect example in doing the will of God. During His earthly ministry He faithfully stuck to His mission, refusing to be sidetracked. The result of this was His heavenly Father's approval, which was spoken out loud three different times in the gospels: at His baptism (Matthew 3:17), on the Mount of Transfiguration (Matthew 17:5), and at the temple prior to His death (John 12:28). As Jesus prayed for Himself before going to the cross, He said this, "I have glorified You on the earth. I have finished the work which You have given Me to do" (John 17:4). That is an amazing statement, actually. Things were worse at that time than they had been during Jesus' entire earthly ministry, especially politically. Yet Jesus could say to His Father that He had finished what He had been sent to do, as far as His earthly ministry went. The only way this statement could be made was with the knowledge that Jesus had the approval and blessing of God, regardless of the political or religious climate.

In the final chapter of the gospel of John we find an interesting vignette between Peter and Jesus that is often overlooked (John 21:18–23). As they stood on the shore of the Sea of Tiberius, Jesus pointedly asked Peter three times if he loved Him. After the third question and Peter's affirmative reply, Jesus made a prophetic statement directed to him. He said the day would come when Peter would "stretch out [his] hands" and others would "carry [him] where [he did] not wish" to go (v. 18). John adds a note in verse 19, explaining to the reader that Jesus was speaking of Peter's death. Jesus' final comment to Peter was, "Follow Me" (v. 22).

It is easy to picture Peter's response if you read the passage carefully. Jesus had spoken a prophetic word to Peter before about his denial, and Peter surely understood more than any other disciple that whatever Jesus prophesied would happen. But instead of thinking about what Jesus had said to him, Peter's eyes fell on John. I can see Peter gesturing toward John as he said, "But Lord, what about this man?" (John 21:21). Jesus's response was that what happened with John had nothing to do with Peter; it was actually none of his business. He pointedly said, "If I will that he remain till I come, what is that to you? You follow Me" (John 21:22). John notes that this saying quickly spread as the rumor that John would not die until Jesus returned.

The whole point of this encounter between Jesus, Peter, and John was Jesus's emphasis on following Him. We can easily fall into the same trap that Peter fell into. We get so distracted looking at the lives and ministries of other people that we lose our focus on following only Jesus. Seeking His applause is our motivation for walking in the way He leads.

This chapter began with a story about Terri, a young woman who desperately sought the approval of others. I hope that those who identify with Terri can realize that no one person can meet all of our emotional needs for acceptance and approval. God has already done that through Christ and His love for us. Romans 8:1 says, "There is therefore now no condemnation to those who are in Christ Jesus." We are accepted and loved by our heavenly Father, who offers us His approval and acceptance through His Son, Jesus Christ.

*Reflection*

---

◆ If you struggle with being a people pleaser, make a habit of asking yourself this question: Am I following God's leading in my life, or am I doing what someone else thinks I should do?

◆ When asked to take on a responsibility, what is your first reaction? Is it to pray about it, or is it to ask others' advice?

◆ Begin to pray daily that in everything you do, your aim will be the bulls-eye of God's approval, rather than someone else's.

# 9

# The Disconnect of Bitterness:
## *Pull It Up by the Root*

*N*othing can unplug a believer from her joy faster than bitterness of heart and her evil siblings: anger, resentment, unforgiveness, discouragement, and jealousy. Someone once said that bitterness does more damage to the vessel in which it is stored than the vessel on which it is poured. There is truth in that statement because it is the harboring of bitterness that can turn a once joyful believer into an angry and unforgiving person.

It isn't possible to separate these siblings since they are so closely related. In fact, you might call them "Siamese Siblings," because they are all connected. It's not so much that one leads to another as it is that they usually coexist as a sinister group.

The book of Acts relates the story of Simon, a sorcerer in Samaria, who asked Jesus' disciples if he could purchase the ability to perform miracles from them. Peter was horrified at this request and rebuked Simon, saying that money could never purchase God's gifts. He demanded that Simon repent immediately and then spoke this prophetic word: "For I see that you are poisoned by bitterness and bound by iniquity" (Acts 8:23). Peter clearly identified Simon's problem as "bitterness," in that he wanted the power that the disciples had exhibited for his own selfish purposes. It can be translated literally from the Greek as, "in the gall of bitterness." This is an idiom meaning "unusually envious of someone."[1] Simon was jealous of the spiritual power the disciples possessed and wanted it for himself. This indicates the self-centered nature of bitterness— it always focuses inwardly and on how one has been wronged.

Biblical principles prove to be true in any setting—personal as well as cultural. A most extreme example of a root of bitterness is found in the never-ending conflict in the Middle East. Since biblical times, the Jews and Arabs have harbored animosity against each other, and the layers of hostility, suspicion, and resentment have only deepened over the centuries. Violence and hatred have become a way of life, and people on both sides see no other solution than the complete annihilation of their enemies.

Recently I watched a documentary called *To Die in Jerusalem*, which explores this conflict from another perspective.[2] It is the story of two mothers with sixteen-year-old daughters (who eerily looked very much alike) living barely four miles apart in Jerusalem. Unwittingly, these young women became symbols in the conflict between their people. Rachel Levy lived in a Jewish neighborhood, and Ayat al-Akhras was from a nearby Arab village. Both shopped weekly for their families in the same Jewish supermarket near their homes. On March 29, 2002, Ayat strapped a bomb to herself and then detonated it in the supermarket, killing Rachel, who was shopping there at the time.

The film is the story of Avigail Levy, Rachel's mother, who eventually attempted to contact Ayat's mother, Um Samir al-Akhras. Avigail desperately sought to understand how a lovely sixteen-year-old girl could be persuaded to become a suicide bomber and not only kill herself, but innocent bystanders as well. Once the two mothers finally met (via satellite), Avigail persistently tried to connect with Um Samir through their common experience, both having daughters who had died violently. Avigail repeatedly asked Um Samir why and how a beautiful young woman such as Ayat could be persuaded to do something so brutal. Avigail was really looking for Um Samir to denounce violence and suicide bombings, but she never got what she so desperately wanted.

After four hours of heated dialogue, Avigail finally gave up. Um Samir refused to renounce the bombing and could not even converse civilly with Avigail. All she could do was angrily denounce the Jews and blame them for the Palestinians' troubles. I found it difficult as a mother to watch the documentary—the emotions were so raw and the anger and bitterness were so thick you could sense it through the television. Um Samir demonstrated the heart and mind of a woman poisoned by bitterness. Her mind and emotions had nowhere to go but her default setting of anger and hostility. I realized once again that I cannot begin to understand the depth of hatred I had just witnessed. The hostility is so entrenched that it is likely the roots of bitterness can never be extracted.

On the other hand, we have dear Palestinian friends who were displaced as children during the Israeli War of 1948. On their mantel in Amman, Jordan, is the set of house keys to the wife's childhood home in Jaffa. Sixty years ago her family fled Jaffa because of impending war, intending to return in a few weeks. But that never happened due to the outcome of the war, and she has told us many stories about the difficulties her family endured in the following years. Her father once traveled secretly to Jaffa just to briefly stand in front of and look at his family's home that had been handed over to an Israeli family. The house keys on the mantel are a reminder of their staggering losses, and they symbolize the plight of the Palestinian people.

I realize this is a rather extreme example, but take note that the most difficult and lasting conflict in our world today is fueled by the powerful force of bitterness, resentment, and intense rage. There is an old saying that bitterness is like drinking poison and expecting someone else to die from it. Bitterness is toxic to a believer's walk with Christ and must be removed as soon as it is recognized. While our emotions may never affect the ones we resent, they will always affect us, especially in the spiritual realm. Bitterness is a natural reaction to a loss or hurt, and if not dealt with, it will cause us to become resentful toward God and man.

## The Poison Root of Bitterness

Everyone is wronged at some time in life. Unfortunately, this is especially true in ministry, as relationships can become strained due to disagreements, misunderstandings, and hurts. This is inevitable since we live in a fallen world and minister in fallen churches full of fallen people . . . including ourselves! If the root of bitterness is not pulled up, our spiritual lives are choked out and we become consumed with our own pain, unable to see the grace or goodness of God.

The writer of Hebrews specifically addresses the danger of a bitter spirit in chapter 12, logically following up on the previous section on holiness and discipline. In the first section of this chapter (vv. 3–11), believers are exhorted to receive the discipline of the Lord, enduring it and receiving it as evidence of the Father's love and because it is spiritually beneficial. In the next section (vv. 12–17), the writer encourages us to not reject the warnings of God and to renew our efforts to live in peace with one another.

Pursue peace with all people, and holiness, without which no one will see the Lord: looking carefully lest anyone fall short of the grace of God; lest any root of bitterness springing up cause trouble, and by this many become defiled; lest there be any fornicator or profane person like Esau, who for one morsel of food sold his birthright. For you know that afterward, when he wanted to inherit the blessing, he was rejected, for he found no place for repentance, though he sought it diligently with tears (Hebrews 12:14–17).

There are several points that should be noted from this passage. First of all, it is our responsibility to seek peaceful relationships with others. We are not to leave reconciliation to other parties, but to initiate it ourselves. "Pursue" in Greek (*dioko*) is in the present active imperative, which means it is a command to take the initiative ourselves in working toward peaceful relationships with each other. This is part of holiness: the restoration and cultivation of relationships. In fact, it is so important that the writer of Hebrews says that no one can see the Lord in us unless we are pursuing loving relationships with others (Hebrews 12:14).

The next phrase, "fall short of the grace of God" (Hebrews 12:15) does not refer to apostasy (renouncing one's faith), but could be better interpreted as "coming behind" in the grace of God.[3] The ESV translates this verse, "See to it that no one fails to obtain the grace of God." If we are not careful, we can become so focused on our own hurts that we fail to lean upon the grace of God. When this happens, a root of bitterness can spring up, causing problems in our spiritual lives. This word picture is also used in Deuteronomy 29:18–20, when Moses warns against serving the pagan gods of the nations, in order that a "root bearing bitterness or wormwood" would not appear. This poison root produces poison fruit, and is thus a warning that the sin of one person could affect an entire nation. Due to our sinful nature, this root often "springs up," meaning that unless checked, bitterness can germinate in our hearts. It can quickly grow and spread its destructiveness into our relationships with others and with God. Bitterness does not just hinder our spiritual growth, but acts as poison—destroying it. Jesus was alluding to this very thing when he said, "For out of the abundance of the heart the mouth speaks" (Matthew 12:34).

An additional point to be made is the admonition that bitterness will inevitably have an effect on others in our lives. When we nurse a grudge or allow resentment and anger to fester in our hearts, it will certainly spill over and influence other people. We usually enjoy others sympathizing with us or taking up our offense against someone who has hurt us. But this is never beneficial, nor is it helpful to the one harboring the bitterness of heart. The word *defile* means to trouble or annoy, and *Thayer's Lexicon* adds that this word "represents the man who corrupts the faith, piety, and character of the Christian church."[4]

> *W*HEN WE NURSE a grudge or allow resentment and anger to fester in our hearts, it will certainly spill over and influence other people.

At one of our churches I became acquainted with a woman around my age whose parents were active in the church. Over coffee one day, I listened to her as she spilled out her anger and resentment over things that had happened in the church previously. (Believe me, if I had known that was going to happen I would have never met her for coffee!) I was taken aback but quickly realized that her views were a direct result of her father's observations and opinions. After deacons' meetings or church services he would go home and vent his disagreements and disapproval with the sermon and church leadership to his wife and children. Of course, this woman's present attitude was one of the fruits of her father's root of bitterness. It was no surprise to me to find out that her siblings had abandoned church the minute they left home. The children had been defiled by the bitterness of their father, and I believe the Bible teaches that one day he will have to answer for that.

The author of Hebrews uses Esau as an example of a person

overcome with bitterness. Esau's story is told in Genesis 25:27–33 and Genesis 27. Jacob, who was Esau's twin brother, plotted to steal his elder brother's blessing, which according to Jewish custom would be given to Esau upon the death of his father, Isaac. One day when Esau came in from hunting, he asked Jacob (who had cooked a pot of stew) for something to eat. Jacob agreed, but only after asking Esau if he would sell him his birthright, which was the first part of the blessing, in exchange for his stew. By shrewdly taking advantage of Esau's impulsive nature and hunger, Jacob set the stage for his ultimate deception. Esau had no spiritual sensitivity and thoughtlessly agreed to Jacob's proposal. His physical hunger at that moment far outweighed the importance of some future inheritance, in his thinking.

With the help of his mother, Rebekah, Jacob was eventually successful in closing the deal by deceiving his dying, blind father into thinking he was bestowing the blessing of the birthright on Esau, when in fact it was Jacob who was receiving it. When Esau discovered that the blessing had been stolen from him, he was heartbroken and outraged. You can hear the anguish in his voice, "He cried with an exceedingly great and bitter cry, and said to his father, 'Bless me—me also, O my father!'" (Genesis 27:34). Needless to say, Esau hated Jacob and determined that as soon as his father died, he would kill him. Rebekah quickly arranged for Jacob to take a journey to her brother's home a long distance away, ensuring Jacob's safety (Genesis 27:41–46).

As you read this story, you can easily spot the other negatives related to bitterness: anger, jealousy, resentment, and unforgiveness. Surprisingly, the story has a very tender conclusion. In Genesis 33 you can read the story about how Jacob and Esau were eventually reconciled. Apparently in this case, time had healed the wound and the brothers were at peace with each other.

The point the author of Hebrews was trying to make in using Esau as an illustration is that his rash decision had far-reaching consequences. By trading his privileges as the firstborn son for physical gratification, he foolishly gave up what was rightfully his. Even his tears and sorrow could not change the outcome. But it was Esau's own fault. He is described in Hebrews 12:16 as a "fornicator or profane person," indicating that he was ruled by his physical desires and ungodly character. By disregarding God's ways, as Esau did, we also can find ourselves in situations where bitterness and resentment rule our lives. This bitterness not only destroys our spiritual walk with God, but can even cause physical illness and depression.

## Causes of Bitterness

I have occasionally said that I could be a really good Christian if it weren't for people. But we are called to work with people, and that means we will always have to work through some of these issues. Sometimes people hurt us unintentionally, but at other times it is deliberate. On other occasions bitterness can be caused by something that God has allowed to come into our lives, for reasons known only to Him. By identifying the roots of bitterness and resentment we can begin to remove them.

Mary Somerville, in her book *One with a Shepherd*, writes honestly about one of her greatest struggles in ministry, which was people leaving their church and going somewhere else in the community. Who can't relate to this example? She explores this topic and is very open about how difficult it is to not take it personally when someone leaves your church. In reflecting on that time, she says, "We have poured our lives into them, maybe even led them to the Lord and discipled them. They are like family."[5] In their case, ten families who were close friends left their church for a larger one. Mary's reaction was to fall into the depths of discouragement, feeling that all their work had been for nothing. As often happens, at the same time her husband was being criticized by the elders in the church. Mary was determined to not let her emotions get the best of her by pushing her into bitterness or depression, which she could see coming. She sought solace and encouragement in Scripture verses and reading biographies of other Christians who had gone through trials, such as Elisabeth Elliot.[6] Mary also tried to see another perspective—that these families were not personally rejecting her husband, but seeking the best church for their families' needs. I do think this is one of our most challenging areas as ministry wives. Refusing to take rejection personally takes spiritual strength, but it eventually brings the blessing of peace of mind and heart.

I have a friend whom I have known for a number of years who went through a devastating ordeal with her church. After being challenged over some financial records, she and her husband found themselves in a very serious dispute and their church began to fracture, much to their great sorrow. It all seemed to happen so quickly, and she found that some of the couples that had been their closest supporters and dearest friends now were their adversaries. They eventually resigned from the church and have moved on to other opportunities that the Lord has provided for them. However, it has been a long road for her, and she has fought bitterness and depression every step of the way. She felt betrayed by those whom she had considered close friends and angry over the injustice her husband and children had to endure. This is where the evil siblings come in again; if anger doesn't get you one day, discouragement and bitterness are waiting in line for their turn. She has worked through her wounds, but it has been a rocky part of her journey.

Recently a friend of mine who is a ministry wife told me about a staff member who was asked to resign by my friend's husband, who is the senior pastor. When the resignation was announced, a group of people approached her husband, demanding to know why this staff member was leaving the church. Unbeknownst to them, he had lost his job due to incredible incompetency. The entire matter had been handled appropriately according to the bylaws of the church, but the pastor was certainly not going to reveal the entire situation to the congregation. My friend and her husband had to remain silent for the good of the staff member and his family. She told me that she still felt resentful over the situation at times, knowing that the criticism and anger could have been avoided if their people had known the whole story. However, sometimes that is not possible, and we must leave it in God's hands. I told her just to give it time—the way news travels in a church, everyone would know the entire story pretty soon anyway. At times like that I remind myself of Proverbs 24:10, "If you faint in the day of adversity, your strength is small."

Sometimes we must face difficulties that are not caused by people, but are providential, which simply means that God allows them. I think of the Old Testament story of Job as an example of this type of loss. Everything was going quite smoothly with Mr. Job and Company until he was unknowingly put through a test of unbelievable suffering with God's permission. If you have read his story, then you know that the entire narrative of the book of Job has to do with the question of evil and suffering. Job's intellectual, theological, and psychological struggle with this issue illustrates the crisis of faith that this genuinely righteous and godly man endured. His overriding question was: Why would God punish a righteous person by taking everything he valued away from him—his children, his possessions, and his health? We know that Job's friends offered their viewpoints (which were no help at all), but Job was not appeased until he gained a personal question-and-answer session with God Himself. Interestingly enough, God actually did not answer a single one of Job's questions specifically. However, Job was apparently satisfied, and God graciously restored his family and wealth, as well as his peace of mind. From our perspective we know the end of Job's story, but we don't have that advantage for our own lives. All we can know now is that God is good and will enable us to walk, or at least stumble, through our trials in eventual victory.

My friend Kathy Ferguson has walked this path and has shared this part of her journey with other ministry wives. Rick and Kathy worked their way through seminary, pastored small churches, and eventually were called to Riverside Baptist Church in Denver, Colorado.

The Ferguson family flourished in that setting, and they were privileged to see God's hand of blessing in their church, which became a significant spiritual influence in their city. But while on a family vacation in July of 2002, Rick was suddenly killed in a car accident. There are no words that can adequately convey the shock, the horror, the grief, and the loss that a family goes through at such a time. Kathy has shared her own struggle in those dark days and years that followed Rick's death. She found herself wrestling with bitterness and disillusionment over the loss of her beloved husband and the father of her three children. As with other ministry widows, Rick's death was not only the loss of a husband and father, but their entire way of life. Kathy has noted Satan often used one thing in particular against her. The fatal accident had occurred on the highway near Hays, Kansas. Years before, their family had spent the night in Hays as they were moving to Denver. She says, "How Satan used that scene against me to suggest that somehow God had not been as faithful to me as we had been to Him! Ridiculous? Absolutely. That thought is a root of bitterness that I cannot allow to remain in my heart." The words of Beth Moore (given to her by her pastor's wife) brought her insight and comfort:

> Satan knows nothing will disintegrate our effectiveness more dramatically than bearing a deep offense toward God. The more we trustingly expose our hearts and minds to God, the deeper the offense can go when we get our feelings hurt at Him. . . . So, the deeper the emotional exposure to God, the deeper the wound can plunge when a servant sustains a hurt. . . . The profound implication is this: God will always offer the grace we need in any tribulation or tragedy not to become bitter; but if we miss it or refuse it, bitterness can become so deeply rooted that many are defiled. . . . Will you miss the grace when the test comes?[7]

We can also become resentful if we let ourselves focus on the successes of other people's ministries, especially if we have experienced failures. A ministry wife once told me, "Nothing has come easy for my husband." He struggled with his seminary education, his first two small churches were difficult, and his pastorate in a larger city was plagued by staff problems and financial challenges. He then developed high blood pressure, no doubt due to all the stress. She told me that she had to constantly work to not be envious of other pastors and ministers who had few problems in their churches and seemed to float happily along. It's not that she didn't want others to be successful; she just yearned for her husband to catch a break somewhere and pastor in a situation that he could truly enjoy, not just endure. In a devotional to a group of ministry wives she wisely observed that sometimes God calls us to hard ministries. The only way we can meet those challenges is by walking day by day in the power of His Spirit, drawing on His endless supply of grace and mercy.

Whatever the cause, bitterness undermines our relationship with God. If it is any comfort, many of those whose stories are in the Bible had some kind of a struggle with bitterness. Cain was angry over God's refusal to accept his offering, Moses became resentful over the way the Israelites treated him, Naomi changed her name to "Mara" (meaning bitterness) due to the losses of her husband and sons, the psalmists David and Asaph frequently brought their complaints before the Lord, and we could go on and on. While everyone must face bitterness at some point, there is no excuse for it to remain.

## The Antidote to Bitterness

An antidote is defined as "a medicine used to counteract poison."[8] It provides a welcome relief or remedy. The Bible is very clear on the antidote for bitterness—it is simply *agape* love, which means a selfless and self-sacrificing kind of love. This love is described in detail in several passages in the New Testament, such as 1 Corinthians 13, Galatians 5:22–23, Ephesians 4:25–32, and

Colossians 3:12–17. While human love is a powerful force and is one of God's gifts to mankind, it cannot begin to touch the love of God, which is described in detail in the passages above. Rick Renner puts it this way,

> *Agape* is a divine love that gives and gives and gives, even if it's never responded to, thanked, or acknowledged. You could say that *agape* love is a love that isn't based on response but on a decision to keep on loving, regardless of a recipient's response or lack of response. . . . It is the highest, most noble, purest form of love that exists.[9]

Jesus, of course, demonstrated this love repeatedly throughout His earthly ministry. When we study through the gospels, we consistently see Jesus's patience, love, and forbearance in His responses to others. I once did a study of the book of Mark for a Bible study I was teaching at the time, and I looked closely at the account of Jesus and the rich young ruler (Mark 10:17–22). Mark comments in verse 21, "Then Jesus, looking at him, loved him." I was struck by the phrase "loved him." As Jesus looked at this man, He saw the frailty of his human condition and lack of spiritual understanding, knowing that this young man would reject Him, due to his love for his possessions. Nevertheless, Jesus loved him unconditionally. In other words, the *agape* love of Christ is not just some kind of mystical, ethereal emotion, but God's love for every single person that has ever lived on this earth.

If you are like me, the descriptions of *agape* love make my heart sink, because I realize how far I am from such a noble thing. But the Scripture tells us that if we are believers in Christ, we have no excuse not to love in this way, "because the love of God has been poured out in our hearts by the Holy Spirit who was given to us" (Romans 5:5). This means that we don't have to work this kind of love up as some kind of a mental or emotional pep rally or scrounge around for it within ourselves. When the Spirit indwells a believer,

He supernaturally gives this *agape* love. I like this view: "God has magnificently bestowed on you sufficient love to be longsuffering in any relationship or situation."[10] It is not our love that is bestowed on others, but it is the love of God revealed through us. Eugene Peterson puts it this way in his paraphrase of Colossians 3:12–14:

> So, chosen by God for this new life of love, dress in the wardrobe God picked out for you: compassion, kindness, humility, quiet strength, discipline. Be even-tempered, content with second place, quick to forgive an offense. Forgive as quickly and completely as the Master forgave you. And regardless of what else you put on, wear love. It's your basic, all-purpose garment. Never be without it. (*The Message*)

Peterson's contemporary language describes *agape* love as a piece of clothing that should be worn consistently, since God has chosen it for us. I don't want to trivialize *agape* love, but I can't help expanding on his word picture. I suggest that this kind of love can be compared to a really good black tank top. (I suspect every woman reading this book gets this analogy.) It can be worn with everything from a suit and pearls to jeans and flip-flops. It always works when appropriately put with other pieces of clothing, and it is a staple in every wardrobe. When I pack to go on a trip, the first thing I throw in my suitcase is my black tank top, regardless of the season or weather. It is always useful in some way. One of my packing rules is, "My black tank top—never leave home without it!" Like the ubiquitous black tank top, *agape* love is always appropriate, always needed, and should be the distinguishing characteristic of a true servant of Jesus.

This is the antidote to the poison root of bitterness. A close reading of the passages that describe *agape* love (listed above) helps us understand the practical demonstrations of this love and how it relates to our relationships with others. But the most important element of this love is forgiveness.[11]

It is interesting that when Jesus referred to forgiveness, He usually added that God would forgive us to the degree that we forgive others. Consider these verses:

- "And forgive us our debts, as we forgive our debtors" (Matthew 6:12).
- "For if you forgive men their trespasses, your heavenly Father will also forgive you. But if you do not forgive men their trespasses, neither will your Father forgive your trespasses" (Matthew 6:14–15).
- "Judge not, and you shall not be judged. Condemn not, and you shall not be condemned. Forgive, and you will be forgiven" (Luke 6:37).

I don't know about you, but I find it very sobering that God will forgive me as I forgive others. This emphasizes the serious nature of forgiveness; it is not an option for the follower of Christ. When there is genuine *agape* love, there will be a forgiving spirit and a greater indebtedness to God for His mercy. "Love and forgiveness set up a chain reaction: The more forgiveness, the more love; the more love, the more forgiveness."[12]

Peter once asked Jesus how many times he should forgive someone who sinned against him (Matthew 18:21–22). Jesus's answer was that Peter should forgive "seventy times seven" (v. 22). Of course Jesus's intent was not to put a numerical value on forgiveness, but to illustrate that the spirit of forgiveness has no limits. In musing over this Scripture one day, it occurred to me that perhaps Jesus' words could be interpreted to mean that there are times when we have to continually forgive the same offense. For those who have been seriously wronged, abused, or victimized, there may have to be a lifetime of continued forgiveness in order to find freedom.

Along with an understanding of *agape* love is the spiritual maturity to accept whatever God has allowed in our lives. I once heard a speaker say that she had fought with God for three years of her life, resisting something that had happened to her. I don't even recall what the fight was about, but I do remember immediately thinking two things. First, where in the world did she get the strength to fight God for *three years?* I cannot even imagine the energy that took. Secondly, if you fight with God, you will lose, end of discussion; there is no other possible outcome. Therefore, use the good sense God gave you and begin to do the serious work of receiving whatever He has allowed into your life. I don't mean to imply that this is easy to do. It is hard work and often takes years, but it is the only way we can truly experience the grace of God and hope for the future. Oswald Chambers says:

> If God has made your cup sweet, drink it with grace; or even if He has made it bitter, drink it in communion with Him. If the providential will of God means a hard and difficult time for you, go through it . . . You must go through the trial before you have any right to pronounce a verdict, because by going through the trial you learn to know God better. God is working in us to reach His highest goals until His purpose and our purpose become one.[13]

Finally, maintaining a heavenly viewpoint helps us manage resentments and bitterness from the past. Sometimes, as in Esau's case, time can give us a greater perspective and put our hurts in the context of time. I remember once seeing a woman at the grocery store with whom I had lost contact. I was genuinely glad to see her, and we quickly caught up as we stood next to the Cheerios and Cocoa Puffs. As we talked, I started to remember why we had lost contact—she had offended me in the past, but I couldn't remember exactly how. By the time I arrived home, I remembered the whole scenario, but for some reason, it didn't bother me. It didn't matter in the larger scheme of things, and there was no reason whatsoever for me to have a broken friendship over something that was really insignificant. The passage of time (and my memory) enabled me to see it from another perspective.

Sometimes we must intentionally work to see our lives from that perspective. Getting from bitterness to *agape,* or at least acceptance, often is a process. I wish we could remove the roots of bitterness after one good "quiet time," but that doesn't always happen. Of course God can do so if He wishes, but it seems to me that it usually takes deliberate choices and some work to pull up those roots.

The writer of Hebrews exhorts us to look carefully to be sure that we do not "fall short of the grace of God" (Hebrews 12:15). It is our responsibility to guard our hearts and minds when we have been wronged. God will deal with others if they have sinned against us, but we are responsible for our own reactions. If we don't pull bitterness up by the roots, making sure all traces of it are gone, it can easily return. But once it is removed, there is space for God to do His work of grace in our hearts.

## Reflection

◆ Do you find yourself always wanting to say something negative about a certain person, situation, or church? Can you examine your heart honestly to determine if you have a root of bitterness?

◆ If you hear that someone who wronged you is being blessed, can you truly rejoice or does it make you angry?

◆ Mary Somerville suggests praying through Philippians 4:4–9 to find God's peace.[14] Rejoice in the Lord by reminding yourself how much He has done for you. Turn on music that ministers to you, or pray through the words of some of the great hymns (such as "How Firm a Foundation"). Ask God to help you depend on His grace for gentleness, patience, truth, and all of the good things that are His gifts. Meditate on these blessings and remind yourself that in your pain you have entered into the sufferings of Christ by not retaliating.

# 10

## The Disconnect of Failure:
### *Failure Isn't Fatal, but It Sure Feels That Way*

Thomas Edison once said, "I have not failed. I've just found ten thousand ways that won't work."[1] Talk about spin! However you want to describe it, failure is the inability to meet certain standards or expectations. Hundreds of books have been written in order to put failure in its proper perspective in the business community. But failure in ministry is a whole other animal, and it can be very challenging to overcome. That's because ministry not only includes the professional dimension of life, but the personal as well. And while a ministry couple can succeed professionally, failure in the family arena can be even more devastating, since our family lives are so much a part of our ministerial lives.

I want to be very honest in this conversation on failure. Much of our Christian language consists of statements about God being the God of the second chance, or that when you fail, you should simply get up and start over again. But in reality, we do not always adhere to such lofty principles. Those who fall short often carry the stigma of failure in the Christian community for the rest of their lives. We need to have a clear understanding of what failure entails and how to view it from a biblical perspective. As a ministry wife, this is especially important, due to the unique combination of ministry, family, and profession.

One thing is for certain—failure knows no boundaries. The Bible is brimming with examples of women and men who fell very, very far from God's standard of righteousness. It should encourage us to realize that God doesn't wash His hands of us after we have failed, but rather He picks us up, dusts us off, and sets us on the path once again. Oh, that people were so gracious! Looking at some observations and examples of failure will hopefully enable us to gain a better understanding of how to manage any failures that come our way.

## Redefining the Terms

Just what is true success in the ministry, anyway? In order to clearly understand our terms, we need to put failure and success in the context of ministry. Success in the kingdom of God drastically differs from success in the world.

Jesus taught that someday we would all have to give an account for the way we have lived. He said to His disciples, "For what profit is it to a man if he gains the whole world, and loses his own soul? . . . For the Son of Man will come in the glory of His Father with His angels, and then He will reward each according to his works" (Matthew 16:26–27). Here is the contrast between the two kingdoms. A person can "gain the whole world" by money, fame, or success, but he can "lose his soul" due to neglect of the things of God. Paul tells us that we will eventually have to stand at the judgment seat of Christ and give an account of our work. That is where the ultimate determination of true success or failure will take place.

Jesus is the example of perfect success in God's eyes. On more than one occasion, God spoke audibly from heaven, expressing His pleasure with His Son (see chapter 8). Obviously Jesus was carrying out the will of God and His mission on earth. As Jesus hung on the cross, He cried out, "It is finished!" (John 19:30), meaning that He had completed His purpose in coming to earth as the Son of Man. However, from an earthly standpoint, Jesus was anything but a success. he was born to peasant parents in a stable and grew up in an insignificant village in Galilee. Later on, when Philip told Nathanael that he had met the Messiah, who was from Nazareth, Nathanael snidely commented, "Can anything good come out of Nazareth?" (John 1:46). Jesus's family had no monetary resources or outstanding business successes, and His education was the same as every other Jewish boy's in the village. In other words, we do not see in Jesus' early years any signs of "worldly success." Yet we know He perfectly fulfilled the will of His Father.

When Jesus was hanging on the cross, the Scripture records that those who passed by scorned Him and laughed at Him (Matthew 27:39–43; Mark 15:29–30; Luke 23:35). This is hard for twenty-first-century readers to understand, it seems so cruel. However, in the culture of first-century Judaism, those who were condemned to death were viewed as receiving their just dues (also called "retributive theology"[2]). They believed that Jesus deserved to suffer and that God was punishing Him for His blasphemy of claiming to be God. From the earthly perspective, Jesus was a colossal failure. But from the heavenly perspective, He was a perfect success. Having paid the price for our salvation, He ascended into heaven from the Mount of Olives and "sat down at the right hand of the Majesty on high" (Hebrews 1:3).

My husband has often defined true success as "finding the will of God for your life and doing it." True success is not measured by earthly standards but heavenly ones. However, we frequently need to remind ourselves of that truth, since we are so easily swayed by our culture and its value system.

## Observations on Failure

Failure in ministry has various facets: not living up to expectations, public and private failure, family failures, failing to take advantage of opportunities, and unwise reactions to failure. We will look at each of these in detail in the following pages.

### The Failure to Live Up to Others' Expectations

A ministry wife frequently has to endure others' expectations of what she should be or do. As we already discussed, those expectations will likely differ according to geographical areas, ethnic traditions, or other factors. But it is the rare wife who can (or even wants to) live up to some of those expectations. Those who preceded you in ministry usually unintentionally set them, and they can be very frustrating.

Some of these expectations are serious in nature, while others are more insignificant. Nevertheless, feeling that you have disappointed someone is not an enjoyable experience. I recently heard a ministry wife tell a story about this very thing. Several years ago a woman in her church gave her a lovely suit that was just her size. She was thrilled with it, and even though her own style was not quite so formal, she wanted to wear it the next Sunday morning. Feeling like this suit called for more than just her normal accessories, she put on her pearls and pumps, feeling like she was quite the well-dressed woman. After the service was over, an older woman walked up to her, put her hand on her shoulder and said, "Well, *now* you look like a pastor's wife!" She was truly speechless and wanted to blurt out, "Well excuse me, what *does* a pastor's wife look like, anyway?" That remark stung. She didn't look right all those other Sundays? And why not? Was there some kind of "preacher's wife dress code" she had neglected to observe? She wanted to say, "Please judge me by my heart, not my clothes!" She laughs about this story now, but she told me that to this very day, she never glances at herself in the mirror before leaving for church without wondering if she looks like a pastor's wife. (I wish we all looked as good as she does!)

On a more serious note, failing to meet the expectations of those whom you love and respect is painful. One of the saddest narratives in the New Testament is when the disciples were not able to stay awake and pray with Jesus in the garden of Gethsemane as He faced His most difficult hour. Every time I read that story, I identify with the disciples, knowing how it is to be physically and emotionally exhausted. Yet, I can only imagine their shame and bitter regret as they later recalled Jesus' piercing question, "What! Could you not watch with Me one hour?" before His arrest and crucifixion (Matthew 26:40). Oh, to have that hour over again and pray with the Lord! Don't you imagine they relived that scene in their minds over and over again? It was a monumental failure and the first of several that would occur in the next few hours.

The contrast between the disciples in the last hours of Jesus' life and their preaching ministry in the book of Acts is completely miraculous. Empowered by the Holy Spirit, and certain of the message they were preaching, the disciples succeeded where they had previously failed, by openly proclaiming Christ, his death and resurrection.

## The Failure to Live Up to Our Own Expectations

A good friend of mine, who is a wonderful ministry wife, went through a difficult time of discouragement with her husband after taking on a new church. As so often happens with a new pastor, there was a flurry of growth due to his arrival and fresh leadership. However, it didn't take long for some of the church members to begin to grumble and say that they preferred "more stable growth." Opposition to his leadership started to intensify, and he frequently heard people say, "I was here when you came, and I'll be here when you leave." (We've heard that one ourselves.) Soon attendance began to decline, and my friend and her husband found themselves in a serious struggle for the survival of the church. Her husband was devastated by this turn of events and was overcome by a sense of failure. He was the pastor, he knew he was gifted for the office, and he loved preaching and pastoring. What was wrong with him? Why could he not lead this church effectively as he had others? Why did his people not respond to him or trust him? These questions and many others haunted this young pastor and led him to believe that he had miserably failed his church, his family, and God.

This so often happens in the Christian world. We know people in the Bible failed, and we know no one is successful all the time, but when it happens to us, it is devastating. Preachers speak about this topic frequently, but they act as if they believe it's not supposed to happen to them! My friend's husband became apathetic, since nothing he did or said seemed to make any difference. He would sit for hours in his office and then call her, saying, "I have nothing to say to my people," which is a preacher's biggest nightmare. Not only did he feel like a failure with his church, but more importantly he felt like a spiritual failure. If he couldn't manage to live in "victory," how could he help any of his church members? Nevertheless, he continued to preach every Sunday; somehow he would pull it off and methodically move on to the next week. The only bright spot in this whole scenario was a pastor friend who faithfully called him every week in order to encourage him. Those calls were the only thing that kept him engaged in ministry to any degree, and some days they were the only thing that kept him from resigning.

Eventually a group of men rallied around this young pastor and took him on a prayer retreat. They ministered to him, prayed with him, and worked toward creating a support system that would undergird his ministry. Slowly but surely my friend's husband began to regain his confidence and his sense of calling. He went on an exercise and diet program that strengthened him physically and emotionally. But most importantly, he rediscovered the joy of the Christian life and the assurance of being in the will of God. It was a slow but steady recovery, but he was able to make it by depending on the grace of God every single day.

> *A* DISCOURAGED husband needs a wife
> to empathize with him and encourage him,
> not to give him spiritual instruction, no matter
> how good her intentions are.

As the wives of pastors, many of us can relate to this experience. We would like to think that we could pray for our husbands and give them Scripture verses written on Post-it Notes that cheer them up immediately. Or we might eagerly share our latest insight from our *Experiencing God* study or remind him of his own sermon the past week. (I have personally tried this, and trust me, it does not work.) A discouraged husband needs a wife to empathize with him and encourage him, not to give him spiritual instruction, no matter how good her intentions are.

My friend has told me that she realized she couldn't help much with the church situation. But she knew she could make an extra effort for their home to be a haven for this weary, discouraged man. She went to extra trouble to make meals he enjoyed and to have close friends or family over to provide companionship. She found excuses for special family occasions, such as football games or holiday weekends. She planned outings just to get him away from sitting despondently in front of his computer, waiting for inspiration that never came. She found creative ways to minister to her husband and to help him find his bearings once again. (I love the resourcefulness of women!) Thankfully their church recovered and has done very well since those days. She has told me how grateful she and her husband are that they did not just pull up and move in order to avoid this painful process. But rather by working through it and facing the challenge, they learned so very much. Her husband has realized that his goals and expectations for himself and their ministry must from now on be in line with God's expectations of him, not his expectations and not the church's. And as always happens, they are now able to minister to others who have similar struggles and assure them of God's loving grace, even in failure.

### Succeeding Publicly, but Failing Privately

Solomon, the son of David and king of Israel, is an example of a man who had stunning public success but failed in his family and spiritual life. Solomon was a builder who constructed the temple his father, King David, had always yearned to build. He eventually erected other exquisite buildings, palaces, and gardens, all of which were stunning in scope and beauty. The book of Ecclesiastes records all of his accomplishments . . . as well as his failures. Early in his life, Solomon was a humble man who sought wisdom from God. His prayer upon taking the throne of Israel, recorded in 2 Chronicles 6, is full of humility, devotion, and gratefulness to God. But once Solomon began to marry foreign wives (for political purposes), his heart changed. Nehemiah's comment on Solomon summarizes his public success but private failure, "Did not Solomon king of Israel sin by these things? Yet among many nations there was no king like him, who was beloved of his God; and God made him king over all Israel. Nevertheless pagan women caused even him to sin" (Nehemiah 13:26).

Solomon is a prime example of a man who succeeded publicly, but failed in the most important area of his life—his walk with God. Solomon illustrates that effective leadership can be undone by a personal life that is undisciplined and ungodly. His final words, recorded in Ecclesiastes 12, indicate that he finally understood that the whole purpose of man was to "fear God and keep His commandments, for this is man's all. For God will bring every work into judgment, including every secret thing, whether good or evil" (Ecclesiastes 12:13–14). Failing to maintain our testimony in our private lives makes our public successes appear very empty. The whole message of Ecclesiastes is that all the glory and success of the world is meaningless without God.

Often a moral failure will bring down a ministry publicly as well as privately. Unfortunately, we have all seen numerous examples of that very thing. However, sometimes wives decide to stay with husbands (or vice versa) and families work to put their lives back together. When that happens, the private pain and betrayal must be dealt with in order for there to be forgiveness and restoration.

*Failure in Parenting*

One of the most difficult aspects of failure is that concerning adult children. The faith (and success) of our children is often considered to be our "report card," or the measurement of our success in matters of faith and parenting. This is especially true for those of us in ministry. When a child deliberately chooses to reject the faith of his or her parents—or make unwise choices that are against their advice—the parents cannot help but feel it is a reflection on them. This is a normal parental reaction and with it comes an enormous amount of guilt, as well as the stigma of failure. After all, we have heard speakers say, "If you fail with your family, you have failed at the most important task of all." But sometimes, despite our best parenting efforts and intense prayer, children may choose another path.

When discussing this with someone, I often use the illustration of an algebraic equation. If you remember algebra (and I've tried to forget it), you know that the answer to an equation is determined by the variable. For example, $2 \times 2 \times y = 8$. The answer (8) indicates that the variable has the numerical value of 2. In terms of people, however, the variable is human nature. A child's human nature—

her choices, friends, influences, education, temperament, etc.—will inevitably alter the answer to the equation.

As Christian parents, we take the task of raising a child seriously. We believe that such things as family devotions, faithful church attendance, involvement in student ministry activities, and Christian education, should guarantee (or equal) a successful outcome. We think our children should always make wise vocational and personal choices that reflect a biblical understanding of life. Proverbs 22:6, "Train up a child in the way he should go, and when he is old he will not depart from it," has been quoted millions of times as a promise to parents. But we know that sometimes this just doesn't happen immediately. Even the most well-meaning and sincere parents can have children who reject Christianity or make choices their parents would never agree with. This can happen even to devout Christians—due to human nature, the variable $x$. When it does, we must remember that our true "report card" will come in the future when we receive our rewards for our obedience and faithfulness.

As parents, we must come to terms with the fact that our children grow up to be independent adults. Those adults have the freedom to choose the way of life they wish. Even though a parent may be heartbroken or terribly disappointed with those choices, we must not let our guilt consume us. There is a point when children must be released and allowed to go their own way. Just because they choose to live life differently does not mean all a parent did was for nothing. Most wayward children eventually return to the Lord after finding that the world's promises aren't so attractive after all. And even if we are still waiting, we should not let those situations rob us of our own joy and obedience to Christ.

King David prayed for his son Solomon as he prepared to take over the kingdom and build the temple. His prayer was, "And give my son Solomon a loyal heart to keep Your commandments and Your testimonies and Your statutes, to do all these things, and to build the temple for which I have made provision" (1 Chronicles 29:19).

God even appeared to Solomon twice, promising him blessings if he would not worship the pagan gods of the land (1 Kings 11:9–11). But Solomon's wives turned his heart away from God. Although he did achieve unparalleled success and riches, his heart was empty. The book of Ecclesiastes is his story of his search for meaning in life. As we already discussed, Solomon eventually concluded the meaning of life could only be found in fearing God and keeping His commandments (Ecclesiastes 12:13). Despite the prayers of a father who desperately loved the Lord, David's son did not follow in God's ways. The bright spot, however, is that Solomon did come to the right conclusion at the end of his life.

I have a friend in ministry who has a heartbreaking situation with her grown daughter. She married a young minister, much to her parents' delight, and moved to another part of the country. One evening my friend got a call from this daughter saying that she was leaving her husband and young son. After determining that there was no physical abuse or serious emotional or mental issues, my friend had to face the fact that her daughter had simply made a terrible choice. She knew that they would all have to live with the consequences of that choice for many years. She has agonized over this situation, but recently told me that despite her daughter's actions, she and her husband are determined to have "a full life" for the remainder of their years. They are involved in a small business and an African mission project along with ministry, and they find it all very fulfilling. They refuse to feel sorry for themselves, and they try not to succumb to the onslaught of guilt and failure that occasionally comes their way. I commend my friend for her healthy attitude every time I see her and I pray that God's grace will continue to minister to her and her husband. And I pray that her daughter will return to her senses!

## Failing to Take Opportunities

The parable of the talents is found in Matthew 25:14–30. Jesus related the story of a man who had three servants and was leaving on a long journey. He gave each servant a certain number of talents, or money, asking that each one of them invest the money or use it in some way that would yield a return. The two servants who were given five and two talents did that very thing, and when the master returned he commended them, calling them "good and faithful servants." But the servant who was given the one talent buried it instead of investing it. When the master demanded an explanation, the servant's explanation was that he was "afraid" (v. 25). The master called him "wicked and lazy," which was quite a contrast to his response to the other two servants (v. 26).

The faithful servants had taken the opportunity given them and had been successful by investing their money in a manner that pleased their master. The other servant, who had risked nothing, failed to even try. He was afraid and lazy, according to the text, thus failing to carry out his master's directive. Within the context of success and failure, the meaning of this parable is crystal clear. When we miss opportunities for ministry, for whatever reason, we fail to do the will of our Master. I know that I have done this myself, simply because I was too tired or uninterested to take the time to reach out to someone or complete a task.

Several years ago we were visiting a church where the pastor and his wife were friends of ours. They had just been at the church a few months when one of the most beloved of all staff members had to resign due to a moral failure. This was one failure nobody saw coming. The church was absolutely devastated, and the new pastor had a delicate situation on his hands. It was very important that he handle this emotional and spiritual crisis in a wise manner. When I asked his wife about it, she said that she didn't know what to say to "these people" in their church. Her solution was to stay in the house for three days, pull the shades, and not answer any phone calls. That way she could avoid dealing with it. As she told me this, I stood there thinking, "You have missed the greatest opportunity you will *ever* have to minister to your people!" At those times, a sympathetic hug or touch can communicate genuine care more than anything else. Times of sorrow, illness, death, and suffering present opportunities for ministry that we must not fail to meet.

## Responding to Failure

Kent and Barbara Hughes have written an excellent book addressing this topic entitled *Liberating Ministry from the Success Syndrome*. The Hugheses have done an enormous service to those in ministry by telling their story with transparency and authenticity. They provide a model for a Christian's response to failure.

After a thriving ministry at their home church in California, Kent and Barbara sensed God's call in planting a new church. With strong support from their mother church and denomination, and with solid financial backing, it seemed like they couldn't lose. According to them, they did everything right. They thought through the demographics, made the necessary arrangements, acquired the favor of the community, and spent time praying for God's direction. Above all, Kent had a good track record in ministry and was entering the prime of his life with energy and purpose. But to their great disappointment, despite all their work, the church did not experience significant growth. After six months, they had fewer attendees than they had when they began. It was that failure that prompted a near breakdown in Kent's life. He began to question everything, even his calling.

Kent makes a very candid confession regarding his misguided desire for success. He writes, "I had bought into the idea that success meant increased numbers. To me success in the ministry meant growth in attendance. Ultimate success meant a big, growing church."[3] He admits that upon examining his heart, he found that he wanted that kind of success more than he wanted the smile of God.[4] Kent writes that he realized he had fallen victim to secular thinking, using the world's standard of success rather than God's. He and Barbara began a serious study of the Scriptures in order to discover anew the biblical principles of success: faithfulness, service, love, faith, prayer, and a positive attitude. Valuing these principles enabled them to find freedom from the "success syndrome."

The positive response to failure is the willingness to learn from it. Although Kent and Barbara did not originally intend to write a book on this topic, they found great fulfillment in sharing this part of their journey with other ministry couples. They set an example for us: Rather than be defeated by failure, we need to face it honestly and seek to learn from it. Rather than make excuses for it, we must evaluate how our own attitudes and actions contributed to it.

Some failures are brought on by our own choices, as well as circumstances. But whatever the cause, failure teaches us things that we would otherwise have never known. We can often find God's redemptive purposes in it. This is the response that brings healing and hope!

### Failing Successfully

It helps to realize that most of our failures are temporary. By learning from them and putting them in the proper perspective, we can avoid making the same mistakes again. Verla Gillmor says, "Treat failure like a visitor: allowed to deliver unpleasant news, but not allowed to take up permanent residence. We need to say, 'Make your point—then leave.'"[5]

On Paul and Barnabas's first missionary journey, they took with them a young man from Jerusalem named John Mark. For some unknown reason, John Mark left them when they were in Pamphylia, presumably to return home (Acts 15:38). When the time came for them to revisit the churches they had established, Barnabas was determined to take John Mark with them again. Paul strongly disagreed and the dispute became so sharp that they parted company. Presumably the merciful Barnabas wanted to give John Mark another chance. We do not know what happened on that journey or in the following years between Paul and John Mark. Years later, however, as recorded in 2 Timothy 4:11, Paul asked Timothy to bring Mark when he came because "he is useful to me for ministry." Somehow John Mark redeemed himself in Paul's eyes, proving himself to be valuable after all. The story of John Mark illustrates that failure does not have to be permanent. Thank God for the Barnabases who willingly give others the opportunity to redeem their failures.

Thomas, one of the twelve disciples, is known as "Doubting Thomas." When the resurrected Christ appeared to the other disciples, Thomas was not present (John 20:24–29). When he heard their report, he refused to believe unless he saw and felt the scars in Jesus' hands and side. When Jesus appeared to him eight days later, his immediate response was "My Lord and My God!" (v. 28). Thomas's failure to believe that Christ had risen was eventually overcome by his faith. Tradition holds that Thomas was successful in taking the gospel to India and dying a martyr's death.

The prophet Jonah is another example of a successful failure. His refusal to answer the call of God and go to Nineveh landed him in the belly of a very large fish. After having some time to think things over, Jonah was deposited on the shore and given the chance to do it all over again. This time Jonah obeyed, preaching repentance to the inhabitants of Nineveh and watching them turn to God. Jonah never quite got over his attitude problem, but to his credit he obeyed the Lord, and to his surprise a city was saved. Jonah also was a "successful failure."

These three examples are men who recognized their failures and were willing to try again. This is the key to successful failure: the desire to succeed for the sake of the gospel is stronger than the desire for self-justification or elaborate excuses.

A.W. Tozer once said, "If it were true that the Lord would put the Christian on the shelf every time he failed and blundered and did something wrong, I would have been a piece of statuary by this time! I know God, and He isn't that kind of God."[6]

Many of God's greatest mission servants have been "successful failures." In the early nineteenth century, Ann and Adoniram Judson sailed for Burma as the first American missionaries to go overseas. Intent on preaching the gospel, planting churches, and translating the Bible into Burmese, the Judsons had only eighteen converts during their first nine years there. Both of their children died of jungle disease before their second birthdays, and finally Ann succumbed as well. Although it took him twenty-four years, Judson's translation of the entire Bible into Burmese was the "foundation stone of Christianity in Burma."[7] The Christian movement in Burma (now Myanmar) began to take root, and today it is home to thousands of churches[8] and more than a million Christians.[9]

The Judsons' mission effort appeared to be an exercise in futility and a total failure during their lifetime. But as the years unfolded, the seeds they had sown reaped an amazing harvest. They are typical of so many missionaries who were and are willing to become temporary failures, in order for the kingdom of God to succeed.

When we have failed—in our eyes, others' eyes, or God's eyes—we must determine to look at our situations through the lens of an eternal perspective. Only then can we respond in the right way and find the strength to start all over again.

*Reflection*

---

◆ What are some expectations you have not met? Were they your expectations, someone else's, or God's?

◆ Ask God for the courage to look at your failures from His viewpoint. Was any part of it your own making? Is there anything for which you need to be forgiven or released? Do you feel guilty for failing at something that really was not your fault?

◆ A friend once sent me this quote when I was discouraged: "Courage does not always roar. Sometimes courage is the quiet voice at the end of the day, saying 'I will try again in the morning.'" Meditate on Isaiah 30:15, which complements this quote.

# 11

# The Disconnect
# of Stress Fractures:
## *Pressures That Stress Us*

There are certain areas of life that do not demand our full attention, but rather simply annoy us on a regular basis. I call these areas "stress fractures." In medical terminology a stress fracture is "a fracture caused by unusual or repeated stress on a bone."[1] Therefore, stress fractures do not appear suddenly, but instead they occur from repeated trauma.

The topics addressed in this chapter are some issues that we as ministry wives must face on an ongoing basis—the "repeated trauma." They are certainly not unique to the ministry wife culture, nor are they life altering (hopefully). However, they are areas that all of us *will* face at some point. Repeated stress in these areas can lead to problems if we don't have an awareness of how to deal with them.

# Alone@church.com

Being alone is a unique situation that needs to be explored sim‑
ply because it is the usual state of pastors and/or staff wives of a church.
For practical purposes, unlike most married women, you will often
be alone at church. On Sundays, your husband is busy carrying out
his responsibilities, and you are left to fend for yourself. Jackie, a young
friend of mine, told me that she and her husband transitioned from
a secular job to church ministry. It didn't take her long to realize that
when she was at church, her pastor husband was no longer "hers."
She couldn't expect him to be at her side, and sometimes she didn't
even see him the entire morning. Due to his early Sunday sched‑
ule, he couldn't help get children dressed, fed, and delivered to child
care or any of the myriad of things parents have to do on Sunday
morning. Not only that, but he couldn't sit with her in church or
stand around and drink coffee with her, talking to friends. He was "at
work" and this was his "job." Jackie said that once she got that idea
straight in her head (thanks to the counsel of an older staff wife), she
could deal with it, but it did take some adjustment. It wasn't so much
that she didn't have his help as much that it was as she didn't have
his attention.

One young staff wife with babies told me that she parked in
the reserved "Single Mom Parking" on Sundays because she *is* a
single mom on Sunday mornings. She finds that extra organization
the day before helps her eliminate unneeded stress. She also told
me that remembering that she can support her husband by not
complaining helps her keep a good attitude.

After my husband left the pastorate to serve our denomina‑
tion, we joined a different church in our area. We knew people
there, but it is a very large congregation, and often I would sit
through a service and not see anyone I knew. One week O. S. was
away preaching and I was feeling really sorry for myself. I thought,
"Why go to church? No one will miss me—I don't even have a reg‑
ular spot where I sit. And if I do go, I'll be alone and I don't want

to be alone." Of course, I was alone at home, but I was not exactly thinking rationally. In fact, I would say that this was one of the more outstanding pity parties I ever had. I'm sorry no one else was there to appreciate it! I got over it, but it did give me a fresh appreciation for new people at church and the awkwardness they can feel when they don't know anyone. For those who never met a stranger, this topic is puzzling. But for those more private types, or others who aren't so extroverted, this kind of situation can be intimidating. As everyone knows, you can feel very much alone in the midst of a lot of people.

A ministry wife who is at a new church will be very appreciative of an invitation to sit with someone during the worship service. Our daughter Holly is married to a minister who serves on a church staff in our area. She has told me that consistently sitting in the same area of the worship center has helped her find a small "community" with which to feel comfortable. Even when David is unable to sit with her during worship, she doesn't feel as if she is alone since she knows those who sit around her. In those settings, you may be surprised to find that some of the most meaningful friendships develop between people who have very little in common such as marital status, age, or background. You may *be* alone at church, but you don't have to *feel* alone.

## I Am His Woman, and He Is My Man!

An inevitable situation that ministry wives usually have to deal with at some point is the matter of other women. Christian women, especially those with husbands who are not spiritually strong or not even Christians, will often have a physical attraction for a pastor, ministry leader, or church staff member. There are various reasons for this, but they are irrelevant here. I simply want to address how to handle this kind of situation.

It never ever ceases to amaze me how blatant and obvious some of these women can be, trying just about anything to get the personal attention they want. (I'm sure every single reader has a story that could be added at this point.) Any minister who has a degree of reputable training will have been advised to never counsel a woman alone or allow himself to get into a compromising situation. The best procedure for counseling is to have his wife or another woman (such as his administrative assistant) join the counseling session, or better yet, ask her to meet with his wife. This can help him quickly find out the counselee's true motivation!

There can be some strange dynamics at work in this situation. Sometimes a woman that befriends you can be the same one who is unusually interested in your husband. Most wives pick up on this quickly and set boundaries with the friendship, which is a wise thing to do.

When I first faced this, I confided in an older woman who was a trusted friend and who never failed to give me excellent counsel. I can still hear her saying, "You are his safeguard. You are his protection, and it is your responsibility to help him in this situation. Stand with him at the front of the church, walk to the car with him, and make your presence known. You don't need to say anything to this woman, just be with him. He needs you—his wife—to help him in this awkward situation." Her advice made me see this through a different framework. Rather than get angry at my husband (it wasn't his fault), I needed to redirect my emotions and use that energy in establishing and enforcing some boundaries regarding women and their behavior toward my husband. I also realized that I didn't have to say anything to her at that point; my behavior would send a message.

Thinking about the situation from this perspective helped me enormously. I became more observant and maybe not so naïve when it came to other women. I also realized how eager Satan is to bring temptation and discontentment into our personal lives, and how we must always be on guard. No one is exempt from such a thing. We need to remind ourselves that we stand united with our husbands against anything that might come between us or harm our testimony or commitment to Christ.

An experienced ministry wife spoke at a workshop I attended when I was a young wife, eager to learn from anybody and everybody. She wisely gave this counsel: There are many things that other people can do for your husband—administrative things, sermon research, ministry duties, etc. However, as his wife only *you* can do some things for him—caring for his physical needs, emotional needs, listening to him, being his sounding board, facilitating a good relationship between him and his children, and praying for his personal spiritual journey. All of those things are the privileges of a wife and a wife alone. I honestly cannot say how many times I have remembered that statement over the years, and it has never failed to keep me thinking straight.

It is very helpful to be open with each other on this issue and to have good communication. My husband and I have been "on the same page" in this area and have enjoyed almost four decades of faithfulness to each other, for which we are very grateful.

## Workin' Nine to Five? If Only!

The number one problem for most ministry families is time pressures. Every survey I have seen has this in common. One survey (that I think is typical of most ministry families) indicates that the composite ministry wife is employed at least part time, plus works as much as twenty hours at the church a week, with her husband working around sixty hours a week.[2] That translates into very few hours for family or couple time.

The availability of the minister due to cell phones and email has pushed this issue to the forefront of ministry families. On top of that, the demands on a pastor's time are not the normal demands of a nine-to-five job. Ministers must work Sundays (the day of rest?), weekends, various evenings, and don't forget Christmas Eve and Easter. All of this translates into fewer convenient or "normal" hours for family time.

In the past, when a family went on vacation or even out for a meal together, they had one another's full attention. Those days are over, never to be seen again. One wife told me that on their family outings her husband is always distracted because he constantly answers emails or text messages the minute he receives them. He knows that responding immediately will mean less time later in front of the computer, but it is very frustrating to his wife. I suspect this is the norm in most ministry families in our culture. For women married to student, collegiate, or singles' ministers, the time pressures are even more critical. There are always numerous social activities that must be overseen or some need that has to be met immediately. Inevitably, those events will cut into our personal or family times. One woman told me that she was trying to accept that there are nights when her husband must be at the church on "her time." She struggles occasionally with feeling slightly resentful when he leaves her with their two young children to go to a social event that she would love to attend. He always wants her to go with him, but with young children, it's not always possible. However, she recognizes this is part of ministry life, and she is working to adapt to it. Realizing that her children will not always require so much time doesn't bring much comfort when she is missing her husband.

It almost always falls to the wife to find the time for a couple or family to be together. Women can always sense the need for time alone as a couple or when the children need time with their dad. And of course those times are not convenient. The calendar will not suddenly present the perfect time to spend together as a family, so you have to make those times happen by planning and looking for opportunities.

It also will fall to the wife to communicate her concerns with her husband regarding their schedules. Often husbands become frustrated with their wives because they "just don't understand how much pressure there is." Choosing the right time to talk about the demands of the calendar and having a gracious attitude will help your husband "hear" you. I seriously doubt if there is one minister who intentionally ignores his family, but without realizing it, he can do that very thing.

Not only do ministers have time pressures, but so do their wives. It's not easy to find extra time in most wives' schedules. Can you relate to Marlene's dilemma?

> I really have to sit down and plot my time out. I have boys who are active in sports so I have to schedule my time and decide what is a priority. Right now my boys are a priority. It's really hard to juggle time. I have to make time for my husband, I have to make time for my children, and I have to have time for household stuff—all outside of work time. My work time is scheduled for me, sports time is scheduled for me, and Sundays at church are scheduled for me. So I have a lot of scheduled times—it's the time in between that I have to use wisely with my family and with my church.[3]

No wonder ministry wives and moms get frustrated when it comes to managing time. Like Marlene, we often only have little snippets of time here and there, rather than hours on end. Nevertheless, God has promised to "supply all [our] need according to His riches" (Philippians 4:19).

There is a more basic issue relating to this topic: understanding the principles of time management. Integrating these principles into our lives will not only help us accomplish what we need to do, but also make time for family or couple togetherness. There are many resources on this topic—Christian and secular—that can be very helpful.

Charles Hummel wrote a classic little work in 1967 entitled *The Tyranny of the Urgent*. He begins by explaining the Parkinson's Principle: "Work expands to fill all the available time."[4] I would adapt this by saying that "life in ministry expands to fill all the available time!" None of us seem to have the time that we need in order to accomplish our tasks. What is our problem? Hummel writes, "We live in constant tension between the urgent and the important."[5] He goes on to explain that the important tasks such as Bible study, prayer, ministry, and service (things with eternal value) can be put off. They do not call for an immediate response. However, the urgent tasks of everyday life demand our attention, and we always acquiesce to them.[6] Without realizing it "we've become slaves to the tyranny of the urgent."[7] To illustrate, write down the things in your life that you consider the most important. Then look at your calendar and compare the way you have spent your time in the last few weeks with your list of important things. It is easy to see our inconsistencies—we don't give the greatest part of our time to the important things; it's the urgent duties that fill up our lives.

Hummel points out that no one had more work to do than Jesus, and He only had three short years to complete His mission. Yet He never failed to spend time with His Father in prayer, giving the important tasks priority over the urgent ones, which were the needs of the disciples and the crowds. The thrust of Hummel's message is to regain control of your time by reconsidering your activities in light of the important and the urgent. He points out one truth that hit me especially hard the first time I read this small book. In discussing accepting invitations or taking on a task, he suggests that we first simply look at our schedule. If it is too full and we do not feel any particular leadership toward this responsibility, then we just say, "No, thank you." He makes this point: "I have never heard the answer, 'We are sorry that because you couldn't come, we had to cancel our plans.' I have come to realize that I am the indispensable person *only until the moment I say no.*"[8] Hummel gives some practical ideas for budgeting your time so that the important things of life can have their rightful place.

There are no simple solutions to the time challenge. There is little we can do to alter the time constraints on our husbands' jobs. But we can find practical ways to implement our tasks within the bounds of our biblical priorities. Sometimes our problem is not that we are trying to do too much, but rather we are using our time inefficiently. If we make some adjustments in our own schedules, hopefully we will be able to find unexpected times for family. It's also important to have realistic expectations. C. J. Mahaney says, "Only God gets His to-do list done each day. We are not God. We are finite creatures with serious limitations."[9]

I am amazed that even at my stage of life as a grandmother, I still have to work at managing my time. It is so true—work expands to fill all of our time. But God can give us the wisdom and resourcefulness to manage it in a way that meets our needs and the needs of our family. "See then that you walk circumspectly, not as fools but as wise, redeeming the time, because the days are evil" (Ephesians 5:15–16).

These stress fractures will always be with us, no matter where we live, the size of our church, or our stage of life. By prayerfully thinking through how we handle them, hopefully we can avoid any serious injury or pain.

*Reflection*

CHARLES HUMMEL suggests several ways to escape from "the tyranny of the urgent":

◆ First, do not neglect to pray and ask God to help you determine what is truly important for the day ahead of you. Jesus often got up early and spent time in prayer alone with His Father (Mark 1:35). Because of that, He had a clear understanding of the goals He wanted to accomplish. Read the story of Mary, Martha, and Lazarus in John 11:17–34. The urgent need was to prevent the death of Lazarus, who was very ill. But the more important thing was to raise Lazarus from the dead, thus illustrating the power of Christ over death. It must have grieved Jesus to see his dear friends so brokenhearted, but He knew it would be the occasion of His proclamation, "I am the resurrection and the life" (John 11:25.)[10]

◆ Decide what is really important to you.[11] Prayerfully set specific goals, and then determine the objectives that will get you there. Objectives help you determine your goal. For example, your goal may be to get up extra early for your prayer time. How will you accomplish that? By your objectives: being sure your alarm is set, getting the coffee ready to brew, and collecting your materials.

◆ Look over your calendar, and see where you may be wasting time. If you enjoy reading blogs or wandering around the Internet, you know how easy it is to lose track of your time. A friend of mine gave me some good advice when I started graduate school. She advised me to budget the hours I planned to spend on a particular project, and when it was completed, move on to the next thing. If she had not passed this helpful information on to me, I could still be working on my first paper! I found this principle to be very helpful in other areas of my life as well. Find out where your time goes and be brutally honest with yourself. "There is an insidious tendency to neglect important tasks that do not have to be done today—or even this week."[12]

◆ Realize that if you accept an unexpected task, some other activity or responsibility will have to be adjusted.[13] Is it worth it?

◆ Finally, don't give up. We all live in the tension between the urgent and important. I doubt if any of us ever totally master this challenge, but we can certainly make improvements and change our approach to our daily schedules. "Nothing substitutes for knowing that on this day, at this hour, in this place, we are doing the will of our Father in heaven. Only then can we contemplate in peace so many unfinished tasks."[14]

# PART 3
## The Reconnection

**RECONNECTION:** to connect again or anew[1]

# 12

# The Reconnection:
## Our Received Ministry

$\mathcal{O}$ur final conversation on connections in the life of the ministry wife is looking at it from the heavenly perspective. This reconnection is made by recognizing that our ministries are gifts from God and seeking to fulfill them with joy. Despite the disconnects, which are part of life, we are forever connected to Jesus, who walks with us every step of the way.

Jack Taylor, a long-time family friend, first introduced the idea of a "received ministry" to my husband and me. His preaching and his early books on triumphant living were foundational to us in our beginning days of ministry. One of many things he taught us was that a true ministry is "received," not "achieved." In other words, a received ministry seeks the praise of God while an achieved ministry seeks the praise of man. A received ministry is a gift from God, but an achieved ministry is accomplished by human effort.

Paul clearly indicates that since we have received a ministry from the Lord, we must work to fulfill what was given to us.

Every believer has a ministry to carry out according to Ephesians 4:7: "But to each one of us grace was given according to the measure of Christ's gift." A "ministry" is not only for one who is called vocationally, but is God's design for all believers. "As each one has received a gift, minister it to one another, as good stewards of the manifold grace of God" (1 Peter 4:10). Elisabeth Elliot says:

> Each Christian is a dispenser. God has supplied each one with gifts He has selected (He does not offer an array of options), with the good of all in mind. When we imagine that these gifts are for our own mere satisfaction, we are forgetting they are intended for service. All that I have is meant to contribute to the needs of others, and what I need will be supplied through God's dispensers. Thus He unifies and harmonizes the whole church, which is His body, making each dispenser *indispensable*, for each dispenses a grace which is peculiarly His.[1]

One of the leaders in the church of Colossae was Archippus, whom Paul called a "fellow soldier" in Philemon, verse 2. At the end of his epistle to the Colossians, Paul sent his greetings to the church, with this personal note: "And say to Archippus, 'Take heed to the ministry which you have received in the Lord, that you may fulfill it'" (Colossians 4:17). In this short verse, Paul offered the principle that true ministry is received from the Lord; it is not created by the accomplishments of man. Archippus must have needed encouragement or exhortation to continue—or persevere—and to do whatever God had called him to do. As we examine what it means to have a received ministry, we will look closely at this verse.

In this conversation regarding ministry in general, let's think bigger than twenty-first-century churches and parachurch ministries. In light of Christian history, God has used "dispensers" (to use Elisabeth Elliot's word) to accomplish His work throughout the last two thousand years. Of course, there are ministers, evangelists, pastors, missionaries, and all of the traditional roles Christian leadership has taken. But there are also many others—especially women—who have had limited public opportunities but have found ways to express their faith and encourage others to follow Christ.

I once wrote a paper on "Women Devotional Writers in the Church." That is probably the only paper I have ever written that I was not eager to finish! I was so blessed as I researched the women who have had such a lasting influence on Christianity.

For example, Julian of Norwich and Teresa of Avila were medieval mystics who wrote extensively on their personal relationships with Christ, which was very unusual during that historical period. Jeanne Guyon, who lived in late seventeenth-century France, wrote about her simple faith in Christ and courageously challenged the corrupt church of her day. Frances Ridley Havergal, a refined nineteenth-century Englishwoman, wrote beautiful poetry and devotionals, penning the words to several well-known hymns such as "Take My Life and Let It Be" and "Like a River Glorious."

One of the stories that I found most touching was of Lettie (Mrs. Charles) Cowman, who wrote two of the most popular devotional books of the twentieth century, *Springs in the Valley* and *Streams in the Desert*. The Cowmans were missionaries to Asia for sixteen years until Charles became seriously ill. Discouraged and heartsick, they had to return home, where Lettie cared for Charles until he died six years later. During those years, however, Lettie collected devotional material and eventually published the two devotional books. Her writing is borne out of the heartache of losing her husband and the deep disappointment in their broken dreams of giving their lives to missions. Who could have imagined that an obscure woman during the 1920s such as Lettie Cowman would pen two of the bestselling devotional books of the twentieth century, giving a response to the anti-Christian diatribes of the day?[2]

All believers who are willing to give all to Jesus will find that they have a "received ministry"—an opportunity for ministry that is a gift to them. The women mentioned above found their voice, their place of service, and the ministry God had prepared for them. They continue to be examples for us today.

## Take Heed!

In Colossians 4:17, Paul exhorts Archippus to "take heed" to the ministry God has given him. The term "take heed" simply means to pay attention to, find, or discern. The NLT translates it this way: "Be sure to carry out the ministry the Lord gave you." The NIV says, "See to it that you complete the work you have received in the Lord." This language suggests that there is a personal responsibility involved here. The one who is doing the ministry must make the effort for it to happen.

This means that sometimes our best opportunities for ministry are right in front of our faces. Why do we tend to think that we are not really doing the will of God or authentic ministry until we sail for overseas mission work? We have our own personal mission field in the children God gave us to raise. Often those that live or work next to us are the ones to whom God expects us to minister.

There is another point that needs to be made here. As we take heed to the "small things" relating to ministry, God will entrust us with greater responsibilities (see Matthew 25:21). Amy Carmichael, famous missionary to India, is a good example of this very thing. As a teenager in Ireland, on her way home from church on a Sunday morning, Amy noticed an old woman struggling along the street. She was carrying a heavy bundle that was causing her to stumble and fall. Amy and her brothers approached the woman and offered to help carry her bundle of dirty rags. While helping her slowly down the street, Amy was suddenly impressed with a Scripture verse from 1 Corinthians 3:13, which says that on the judgment day, our true work for Christ will be revealed. That afternoon Amy began to seriously consider how to help the less fortunate in her area of

Belfast. She soon began to gather children for neighborhood Bible classes. She began to organize prayer meetings and another Bible class for the "shawlies," poor mill girls who were too poor to buy hats and used shawls to cover their heads.[3] Amy continued to find opportunities to reach out to the poor in her city, eventually feeling the call to foreign missions, particularly India. Amy spent the rest of her life there, teaching, evangelizing, writing, and courageously rescuing young girls from being sold into temple prostitution.

Amy had proven herself faithful in the small things, "taking heed" to her ministry to the poor in Belfast, and doing it with purpose and excellence. No wonder God entrusted her with one of the greatest ministries in mission history, the establishment of the Dohnavur Fellowship in India. "She understood like few others that in order to invest gold in the kingdom of God, sometimes the Sunday clothes must get dirty, the Sunday sentiments must get ruffled, the Sunday occupations must become whatever God places in your hand to do that day."[4]

When my husband and I married, O. S. was serving on staff at the Sagamore Hill Baptist Church in Fort Worth, Texas, under Dr. W. Fred Swank. Brother Swank, as we called him, was an energetic, bombastic figure who understood ministry very well. He used to say, "If you think you are too big for a small job, then you are really too small for a big job." The willingness to serve in a small place and get your hands dirty (figuratively speaking) is the first step toward "taking heed" to the ministry God has put right in front of your face.

## A Ministry from the Lord

Anything that is received has been transmitted from one party and accepted by another. All ministry belongs to God and is gifted to us by Him. The word *ministry* in Colossians 4:17 is *diakoneo* in Greek. The *Key Word Study Bible* defines it this way: "Every business, every calling, so far as its labor benefits others is a *diakonia*.

Therefore, *diakonia* is an office or ministration in the Christian community viewed with reference to the labor needed for others ."[5] In other words, ministry is service to others, whatever form it may take. God has chosen to accomplish His work in this world through His people, by giving them spiritual gifts, natural abilities, and opportunities for service.

When Paul was leaving for his final journey to Jerusalem, he met with the believers from the church at Ephesus to tell them good-bye. He had been warned that he would meet persecution in Jerusalem, but Paul was convinced this was God's will for him. In response to the threat on his life, Paul said, "But none of these things move me; nor do I count my life dear to myself, so that I may finish my race with joy, and the ministry which I received from the Lord Jesus, to testify to the gospel of the grace of God" (Acts 20:24). Paul recognized his "received ministry" was designed and determined by God, and his desire was to complete it with joy.

*G*OD HAS CHOSEN to accomplish
His work in this world through His people,
by giving them spiritual gifts, natural abilities,
and opportunities for service.

Chuck Colson, the founder of Prison Fellowship, wrote *Loving God,* which is a collection of powerful stories of men and women who exhibited an authentic love of God and service to Him in their lives. One year Colson began to receive letters from Myrtie Howell, an elderly woman in Columbus, Georgia. Myrtie was a pen pal to seventeen prisoners she had found through Prison Fellowship, and she frequently wrote to Chuck, telling him all about her prisoners. A year or so later, he was speaking at a seminar in Columbus and paid a visit to Myrtie Howell in the nursing home where she lived.

According to Colson, when he walked in the door, his heart sank at the depressing scene. Rows of elderly people in wheelchairs were staring at a blaring television set, the furnishings were worn, the smell was nauseating, and the carpet was threadbare. After finding his way to her tiny room, Colson was greeted enthusiastically by Myrtie and listened to her story. Myrtie was from a very poor family and had known many losses at an early age. Her age, declining health, and lack of resources had moved her into this home, resulting in a time of spiritual depression in her life. She began to pray that God would give her something to do for Him, if He wasn't going to take her to heaven anytime soon. Colson said Myrtie felt impressed that God wanted her to write to prisoners.

Not having had much of an education (and knowing nothing of Prison Fellowship), Myrtie was hesitant, but she went ahead and sent a letter to the Atlanta Penitentiary, with a request that it be posted on a bulletin board. The letter identified her as a grandmother who loved and cared for people "who are in a place you had not plans [sic] to be."[6] What a response she got! Immediately Myrtie received the names of eight prisoners who were eager to write to her. At the time Colson wrote *Loving God*, Myrtie had written to hundreds of inmates, sometimes over forty at a time. She received letters from prisoners' wives, children, and other family members pouring out their hearts and requesting prayer. She told Chuck, "When I get a letter, I read it, and when I answer it, I pray: 'Lord, You know what You want me to say. Now say it through me.' And you'd be surprised sometimes at the letters He writes!"[7]

Colson was absolutely amazed at Myrtie's spirit and the ministry this elderly woman had found. Colson connects the theme of his book with his visit with Myrtie. He says, "God gave me the final link in my search to learn what loving God really means: Myrtie Howell. To believe, to repent, to obey, to be holy, to bind up the brokenhearted, and to serve. Myrtie Howell knew all about *loving God*."[8]

This is an illustration of a woman who "took heed" of the small opportunity she was given and willingly accepted it. What a gift God gave to her in her received ministry! What a gift hundreds of prisoners found in one lonely grandmother who prayed faithfully for them. These kinds of ministries are most often off the radar screen, as far as the world is concerned. But God takes note, and Myrtie will one day be richly rewarded for her faithful service. Surely if someone like Myrtie can find her "received ministry" in the midst of such dismal circumstances, you and I can as well. God has something for each one of us to do that uniquely fits us.

There is one more important point to make regarding the stewardship of our ministry. Whatever form a ministry takes, we must develop our skills and knowledge to do it well. Paul said in Ephesians 4:12 that our spiritual gifts are given to us "for the work of ministry." Make no mistake, ministry is work. We should never stop learning or studying, in order to improve the quality of our work and to build up our knowledge in Christ. However, this does not mean that in order to be used fully by God in a teaching ministry, for example, that there must be formal training in order to be effective. More than once I have heard that unless one has a working knowledge of the biblical languages or a detailed understanding of church history or systematic theology, that is not really qualified to teach the deep truths of the Word of God. True, this kind of expertise is very helpful in understanding the difficult texts, and everyone who teaches the Word of God should do all they can to master the hidden truths of Scripture. But the Bible is easily understood in regard to what it means to believe in Christ and to follow Him and serve Him.

John Piper points out that the gift of illumination comes through meditation,[9] according to 2 Timothy 2:7, which says, "Consider what I say, and may the Lord give you understanding in all things." The plain meaning of the text is more than anyone can fully understand, much less do. God, in His goodness, has made spiritual truth very clear to us. "The secret of the Lord is with those who fear Him, and He will show them His covenant" (Psalm 25:14). There are thousands of lay Sunday school or Bible study teachers in churches around the world who have no formal theological training, but who faithfully teach biblical truth to toddlers, children, students, and adults. Armed with the Scripture and led by the Spirit, they diligently teach the Word, and He uses it as He will. "So shall My word be that goes forth from My mouth; it shall not return to Me void, but it shall accomplish what I please, and it shall prosper in the thing for which I sent it" (Isaiah 55:11). Ancient theologian Jerome once said, "The Scriptures are shallow enough for a babe to come and drink without fear of drowning and deep enough for theologians to swim in without ever reaching the bottom."[10]

## Fulfilling the Ministry God Has Given You

Paul encouraged Archippus to fulfill his ministry, which means to complete it, to carry it through to the end, or to accomplish it. Paul alluded to this in 2 Timothy 4:7, which was his parting testimony to the early church. "I have fought the good fight, I have finished the race, I have kept the faith." His use of the athletic metaphor illustrates his idea of finishing the race with endurance and faithfulness.

In *My Utmost for His Highest* Oswald Chambers writes, "Have you received a ministry from the Lord? If so, you must be faithful to it—to consider your life valuable only for the purpose of fulfilling that ministry. . . . We each have to find a niche in life, and spiritually we find it when we receive a ministry from the Lord."[11]

I think this is another aspect of what Paul meant—that he had done everything he knew to do. He did "the work of the ministry" with all his heart, taking advantage of every opportunity he had to proclaim Christ with no regrets.

As wives, our first and foremost ministry (besides our relationship with Christ) is to our own husbands and children. If we have chosen to marry and have children, then this commitment is the highest priority. Fulfilling that ministry daily means to care for your husband and children physically, emotionally, and spiritually. It is true that some days that particular ministry doesn't feel so fulfilling! But we don't base our commitment on our feelings, but rather on God's Word and our obedience to it.

Our own personal ministry must be fulfilled as well. As we have discussed, your own ministry may adapt somewhat according to your stage of life, place of service, or type of ministry. Nevertheless, it is our responsibility to "take heed" to our ministry and then do it to the best of our ability.

There are several things, however, that can prevent us from fulfilling our ministry or finishing our race. The most obvious one is disobedience. One of the saddest stories in the Bible is of Saul, the first king of Israel. Saul was a tall, good-looking man (see 1 Samuel 9:2) who was chosen by God to rule over Israel. But Saul could not seem to obey God or listen to the prophet Samuel's counsel. In the battle against the Amalekites and King Agag, God clearly directed Saul to spare no one (1 Samuel 15:1–26). However, Saul thought he had a better idea in sparing the king and the best of the livestock. Samuel was appalled at Saul's disobedience and announced sorrowfully that God had rejected him and would remove the kingdom from him. Saul lost his opportunity to lead the nation and thus fulfill God's purpose for his life because of his disobedience. It is true that when we disobey, there is grace for us. But there are also consequences, and some of those consequences may be lost opportunities for ministry that can never be reclaimed.

Spiritual indifference can also prevent us from fulfilling our ministry. Of all the obstacles that may keep us from an intimate walk with God, this is the most dangerous. Sometimes exhaustion, disappointment, the stresses of ministry, or neglecting our spiritual life can cause our hearts to grow cold and indifferent. This apathy causes us to "drift away" from faith and spiritual truth. As a result, we often end up somewhere far away from the things of God.

When I was a child, our family frequently went to the lake on summer weekends to enjoy swimming and skiing. We would set off to find a cove on Lake Travis where we could secure our boat, picnic, and swim. I remember very well playing "King of the Raft" with my dad, brother, and sister, which basically amounted to all of us trying to drown each other. After we were exhausted from this game, we always found ourselves quite a distance from our cove and our boat, because we had drifted downstream. Of course, this was fine with my brother, sister, and me because we always secretly hoped we would float by "Hippie Hollow," where all the Austin hippies regularly skinny-dipped. I'm sure my parents had already thought that through and always headed for an area as far away from Hippie Hollow as possible. But this is what happens in our spiritual life also. If we don't tend to our devotional life, we can also drift away from the things of God without realizing it. Neglect dulls our spiritual senses. Perhaps that is why the writer of Hebrews said, "Therefore we must give the more earnest heed to the things we have heard, lest we drift away" (Hebrews 2:1).

In Revelation, Jesus addressed the church in Laodicea and charged them with "lukewarmness." He said, "I know your works, that you are neither cold nor hot. I could wish you were cold or hot. So then, because you are lukewarm, and neither cold nor hot, I will vomit you out of My mouth" (Revelation 3:15–16). I have heard that the true opposite of love is not hate, but indifference. Halfhearted service is not service at all and will prevent us from fulfilling the ministry God has given. Of all the obstacles that may keep us from a full life with Christ, this is one of the most dangerous, in my opinion.

An authentic conversation on spiritual lives must include the disappointment we experience when our prayers are not answered as we wanted or life presents us with a difficulty we never anticipated. This disappointment can sometimes cause us to not even want to pray or to question God and His goodness. It can definitely become a roadblock on life's journey. I don't gloss over this question because I have struggled with it myself more than once. One of those struggles was when my father died of cancer at the much-too-young

217

age of sixty-four. He was an unusually gifted man with an enthusiasm for everything from gospel music to politics to his men's Sunday school class to jogging to ranching to University of Texas athletics. He was witty and playful and a delightful grandfather to his five granddaughters. Everyone in our family assumed he would be like his mother and live to be one hundred years old. But that didn't happen, and after a short but valiant battle with cancer, he died at home surrounded by his family. My question was not why he had to die so young. Many fathers die much younger than he did, and all of us will die at some point, anyway. But looking back on that time, I now see that I had presumed that since my dad was healthy, optimistic, and was doing everything "right" in life, he would automatically be rewarded with a long life. That experience was a rude awakening for me. I realized that despite doing everything "right," life may not turn out as you expected. As one of my friends told me at that time, "*Fair* is not in the Bible!"

Phillip Yancey's book *Disappointment with God* was my lifeline during those days and helped me work through some of my questions and hurt. In his foreword, he says this: "I have found that for many people there is a large gap between what they *expect* from their Christian faith and what they actually experience."[12] An honest exploration of our questions and disappointments as they relate to our faith keep us on track and keep our eyes on Jesus. We also know that those experiences are extremely helpful to us as we reach out to others who are suffering. That whole experience taught me some valuable lessons I pray I never forget as I try to fulfill the ministry God has given me.

The busy nature of life, especially in ministry, also can prevent us from carrying out our ministry purpose. Ironically, this is probably the biggest hindrance to a vibrant spiritual walk. Henri Nouwen says that "being busy has become a status symbol."[13] He points out that most of us are deceived into believing that being busy is a good thing because we think it emphasizes how important we are.[14] Those in ministry are just as susceptible to this ego trip as anyone else. With the overwhelming needs and worthy projects around us, we can run ourselves ragged, as if our involvement determines their success or failure. Oswald Chambers hit the bull's-eye on this issue when he said:

> If you have received a ministry from the Lord Jesus, you will know that the need is not the same as the call—the need is the opportunity to exercise the call. The call is to be faithful to the ministry you received when you were in true fellowship with Him. . . . It does mean that you must be sensitive to what God has called you to do, and this may sometimes require ignoring demands for service in other areas.[15]

This is "easier said than done"; however, I have found it to be very true. There are so many worthy causes! But there is only so much time, and I have found that it is best to be involved in projects that are directly related to my interests and gifts. Staying focused on what God has called us to do will enable us to not just fill our days with things to do, but rather to fulfill the ministry God has given to us.

## Joy!

Paul desired to finish his race with "joy" (Acts 20:24). This, I believe, is the result of fulfilling a received ministry. Yes, there is hard work involved, and yes, there are challenges and people that vex us. But staying true to our calling and walking in obedience to Christ results in great joy.

Jerry Sittser says, "Hard is one thing; miserable is another. We might not always be happy doing our work, but we can nevertheless be joyful, taking 'pleasure in our toil,' as the book of Ecclesiastes charges us to do. Such joy will come from knowing that we are doing something that is suitable to our nature and fruitful for God's kingdom work."[16]

Dr. George Sweeting, former president of Moody Bible Institute, has always been one of our favorite friends. When we lived in Fort Lauderdale, he often preached at our church during the winter months. Dr. Sweeting is a tall, stately man who always had a twinkle in his eye and would cheerfully say to people, "Do you have the joy?" We knew exactly what he meant. It wasn't just *joie de vivre*, but more than that—he had the joy of the Lord. His very countenance reflected the love of Christ, and just being around him always blessed us. The joy of the Lord is not happiness with our current circumstances, but rather the joy that comes from following Him and fulfilling the work He has called us to do. Jesus spoke of this kind of joy, "These things I have spoken to you, that My joy may remain in you, and that your joy may be full" (John 15:11).

This is the reconnection—accepting the ministry God gives to you every day by fulfilling it to the best of your ability. I pray that "the grace of His ministering life" will be lived out in our lives and ministries, to His glory.[17]

*Reflection*

◆ What kind of ministry has God given you? Can you look back and see how God has used your gifts and life experiences to equip you for ministry?

◆ What in your life is most likely to keep you from staying focused on God's call?

◆ Think on this: Jerry Sittser says, "We do the will of God when we fulfill our calling in life, a calling that is uniquely ours, like a set of fingerprints . . . It is part of who we are, of what God has put in us, and of how God wants us to serve his kingdom."[18] Our ministry unfolds before us as we walk with Jesus on our journey, in obedience and faith.

# Notes

## Introduction

1. Quoteopia, "Famous Quotes by Deborah Tannen," http://www.quoteopia
.com/famous.php?quotesby=deborahtannen.

## Part 1: The Connections

1. *Merriam Webster Collegiate Dictionary*, 11th ed., s.v. "connection."

## Chapter 1: The Historical Connection

1. Michael Zigarelli, *Influencing Like Jesus* (Nashville: B&H, 2008), 45.

2. Rachel Zoll, "Role of Pastor's Wife Has Changed Since Ruth Graham's Era," *Christian Post Online*, June 18, 2007, http://www.christianpost.com.

3. H. B. London Jr., and Neil B. Wiseman, *Married to a Pastor's Wife* (Wheaton: Victor, 1995), 22.

4. Tertullian, *Treatises on Marriage and Remarriage: To His Wife, An Exhortation to Chastity and Monogamy*, translated by William P. LeSaint (New York: Newman, 1951), 35–36.

5. Robert A. Baker, *A Summary of Christian History* (Nashville: B&H, 2002), 33.

6. For more information on Reformation wives, read Roland H. Bainton, *Women of the Reformation in Germany and Italy* and *Women of the Reformation in France and England* (Lima, OH: Academic Renewal Press, 2001).

7. Marilyn Yalom, *History of the Wife* (New York: HarperCollins, 2001).

8. Robert E. Webber, *The Younger Evangelicals* (Grand Rapids: Baker, 2002).

## Chapter 2: The Couple Connection

1. Modern version of marriage vows adapted from "The Form of Solemnization of Matrimony," *The 1662 Book of Common Prayer* (Cambridge: John Baskerville, 1762).

2. Oswald Chambers, *My Utmost for His Highest* (Uhrichsville, OH: Barbour, 2000), September 29.

3. *NET Bible*, Genesis 2:18, text note 21.

4. Ibid., text note 22.

5. Kent Hughes, and Barbara Hughes, *Liberating Ministry from the Success Syndrome* (Wheaton: Crossway, 2008), 169.

6. R. T. Kendall, *The Thorn in the Flesh* (London: Clays Ltd, 1999), 206.

7. Ibid., 216.

8. Lewis A. Drummond, and Betty Drummond, *Women of Awakenings* (Grand Rapids: Kregel, 1997), 163.

9. Chambers, *My Utmost for His Highest*, September 29.

10. London and Wiseman, *Married to a Pastor's Wife*, 35.

11. Chambers, *My Utmost for His Highest*, September 29.

12. Hughes and Hughes, *Liberating Ministry from the Success Syndrome*, 167–170.

## Chapter 3: The Children Connection

1. Dorothy Patterson, and Armour Patterson, *Parents in Ministry* (Nashville: B&H, 2004), 12.

2. Donald E. Sloat, *The Dangers of Growing Up in a Christian Home* (Nashville: Thomas Nelson, 1986).

3. See Tim LaHaye, *Why You Act the Way You Do* (Carol Stream: Living Books, 1988), and Florence Littauer, *Personality Plus* (Grand Rapids: Revell, 1992).

4. Tracy Osborne, "Ministers' Children: Needs Defined and a Small Group Proposed" (master's thesis, Regent University, 1992), chapter 3.

5. Wendy Hawkins Hermes and Holly Hawkins Shivers gave permission to use all stories about them in this book.

6. *Encarta World English Dictionary Online*, North American ed., s.v. "mistake," http://encarta.msn.com/dictionary_/mistake.html.

7. Sloat, *The Dangers of Growing Up in a Christian Home*, 74.

8. *Thayer's Lexicon*, s.v. "training," http://www.blueletterbible.com.

9. James C. Dobson, *Hide or Seek* (Old Tappan, NJ: Fleming Revell, 1974).

10. Ibid.

11. Florence Littauer, *It Takes So Little to Be Above Average* (Eugene, OR: Harvest House, 2001).

12. Gary Smalley and John Trent, *The Blessing* (New York: Pocket Books, 1978), 26.

13. Ibid., 27.

14. The Quote Garden, "Quotations about Parents," http://www.quotegarden.com/parents.html.

15. Smalley and Trent, *The Blessing,* 222.
16. Ibid., 223–228.

## Chapter 4: The Friendship Connection

1. Harry M. Wood, "Step by Step," 1927.
2. Wisdom Quotes, "C. S. Lewis," http://www.wisdomquotes.com/000190 .html.
3. Suggested websites: http://www.contagiousjoy4him.com, http://www.gpwn. tv (Global Pastors Wives Network), http://lifeway.com/women (LifeWay Christian Resources).
4. Cindy Dykes, "5 Tips for New Ministers' Wives," www.lifeway.com.
5. *Babylon Online Dictionary,* s.v. "hospitality," http://www.babylon.com.
6. *Latin Wordstock Online,* s.v. "hospes," http://www.classicsunveiled.com.
7. Christine D. Pohl, *Making Room: Recovering Hospitality as a Christian Tradition* (Grand Rapids: Eerdmans, 1999), 16.
8. Ibid., 17.
9. Lauren Winner, *Mudhouse Sabbath* (Brewster, MA: Paraclete, 2003), 43–44.
10. Pohl, *Making Room,* 5.
11. Ibid., 32.
12. Winner, *Mudhouse Sabbath,* 50.
13. *Vines Expository Dictionary of New Testament Words,* s.v. "refresh."
14. Wood, "Step by Step."
15. Colleen Evans, "Friends," *Pastor's Family* December 1997/January 1998, accessed at http://www.parsonage.org/articles/married.
16. Pohl, *Making Room,* 179.

## Chapter 5: The Church Connection

1. Dietrich Bonhoeffer, *Life Together* (San Francisco: Harper Collins, 1954), 21.
2. Spiros Zodhiates, *The Complete Wordstudy New Testament* (Chattanooga: AMG, 1991), 73.
3. For a more detailed study of this passage, see Dorothy Kelley Patterson and Rhonda H. Kelley, eds., *Women's Evangelical Commentary: New Testament* (Nashville: B&H, 2006), 733.
4. Patterson and Kelley, *Women's Evangelical Commentary,* 732.
5. Pohl, *Making Room,* 61.
6. "A biblical type is a person or incident which carries a prophetic significance beyond itself. For example, the sacrificial system of the O.T. was typical, i.e., a prophetic picture of the ultimate sacrifice for sin", *Believer's Study Bible,* (Nashville: Thomas Nelson, 1982), 1892.

7. Grace Chavis was a contributor to *The Woman's Study Bible* (Nashville: Thomas Nelson, 1995). Note her comments on 2 Corinthians 6:14 regarding marriage to an unbeliever.

8. Chambers, *My Utmost for His Highest*, August 31.

9. The word *men* in this verse is from the Greek *anthropos*, meaning men or women.

10. Mary Somerville, *One with a Shepherd* (The Woodlands, TX: Kress, 2005), 239.

11. Verdell Davis, *Let Me Grieve, but Not Forever* (Nashville: Thomas Nelson, 2004).

12. Donald P. McNeill, Douglas A. Morrison, and Henri J.M. Nouwen, *Compassion* (New York: Doubleday, 1983), 14.

13. Gayle Haggard, "Gayle Haggard's Letter," *Rocky Mountain News*, November 5, 2006, http://www.therocky.com.

**Chapter 6: The Personal Connection**

1. Alister McGrath, *The Journey* (New York: Doubleday, 2000), 8.

2. Ibid.

3. Ibid.

4. Ibid.

5. A Scripture song consists of biblical verses or phrases set to music, with no other commentary.

6. McGrath, *The Journey*, 80.

7. Chambers, *My Utmost for His Highest*, August 4.

8. Bruce Wilkinson, *Secrets of the Vine* (Sisters, OR: Multnomah, 2001), 109.

9. Henri Nouwen, *Show Me the Way* (New York: Crossroad, 1999), 14.

10. Patterson and Kelley, *Women's Evangelical Commentary*, 584.

11. Ibid.

12. Andrew Kaufman, "Pastors' Wives Come Togther," *TIME*, March 29, 2007, http://www.time.com/time/magazine/article/0,9171,1604902-2,00.html.

13. Email from Tammi Ledbetter, July 1, 2008.

14. McGrath, *The Journey*, 150.

**Part 2: The Disconnects**

1. *Merriam Webster Collegiate Dictionary*, 11th ed., s.v. "disconnect."

**Chapter 7: The Disconnect of Criticism**

1. ThinkExist.com, "Aristotle Quotes," http://www.thinkexist.com.

2. DoveWithin.com, "Quotes," http://www.dovewithin.com/quotes.htm.

## Chapter 8: The Disconnect of Pleasing People

1. Craig Groeschel, "The People Pleasing Pastor," Swerve website, September 22, 2008, http://swerve.lifechurch.tv/2008/09/22/the-people-pleasing-pastor/.

2. Terri is a composite of several women.

3. Philip Yancey, "A Believer's To-Be List," *Today's Christian*, January/February 2001, http://www.christianitytoday.com.

## Chapter 9: The Disconnect of Bitterness

1. *NET Bible*, Acts 8:23, text note 33, p. 1992.

2. *To Die in Jerusalem*, DVD, directed by Hilla Medalia (Boise: Priddy Brothers and HBO Documentaries, 2007). See also http://www.todieinjerusalem.com.

3. W. A. Criswell, ed., *Criswell Study Bible* (Nashville: Thomas Nelson, 1979), 1753, note on Hebrews 12:15.

4. *Thayer's Lexicon Online*, s.v. *"enochleo,"* http://www.blueletterbible.org/lang/lexicon/lexicon.cfm?Strongs=G1776&t=kjv.

5. Somerville, *One with a Shepherd*, 65.

6. Ibid., 67.

7. Beth Moore, *Voices of the Faithful* (Nashville: Thomas Nelson, 2005), 109–110.

8. *The New Little Oxford Dictionary*, s.v. "antidote."

9. Rick Renner, *Sparkling Gems from the Greek* (Tulsa: Teach All Nations, 2003), 671.

10. Ibid., 672.

11. An excellent resource that takes an in-depth look at forgiveness is Nancy Leigh DeMoss, *Choosing Forgiveness* (Chicago: Moody, 2008).

12. Walter C. Kaiser Jr., Peter H. Davids, F. F. Bruce, and Manfred T. Brauch, *Hard Sayings of the Bible* (Downers Grove: InterVarsity, 1996), 388.

13. Chambers, *My Utmost for His Highest*, November 11.

14. Somerville, *One with a Shepherd*, 67.

## Chapter 10: The Disconnect of Failure

1. The Quote Garden, "Quotations about Failure," http://www.quotegarden.com.

2. Retributive theology views punishment as something the wrongdoer deserves.

3. Hughes and Hughes, *Liberating Ministry from the Success Syndrome*, 29.

4. Ibid.

5. Verla Gillmor, "Facing Failure," *Today's Christian Woman*, May/June 2001, 66.

6. A. W. Tozer, *The Tozer Topical Reader* (Camp Hill, PA: Christian, 1998), 185.

7. Edith Deen, *Great Women of the Christian Faith* (Westwood, NJ: Barbour, 1959), 178.

8. Daniel L. Akin, *Five Who Changed the World* (Wake Forest, NC: Southeastern, 2008), 31.

9. *The World Factbook Online*, s.v. "Burma," http://www.cia.gov.

**Chapter 11: The Disconnect of Stress Fractures**

1. *Dorland's Medical Dictionary for Healthcare Consumers*, s.v. "stress fracture," http://www.mercksource.com/pp/us/cns/cns_hl_dorlands_split.jsp?pg=/pp docs/us/common/dorlands/dorland/four/000042557.htm

2. Janet Ingersoll, Janet Mitchell, and Marilyn Blake, "Trends Among Ministers' Wives . . . Where Are We Headed?" *Heart and Soul Connection Online*, http://www.heartandsoulconnection.com.

3. Jennifer Antonsen, "Moments with Marlene—a Pastor's Wife," *Focus on the Family Canada Online*, http://www.focusonthefamily.ca.

4. Charles E. Hummel, *Tyranny of the Urgent*, revised ed. (Downers Grove: InterVarsity, 1994), 3.

5. Ibid., 5.

6. Ibid.

7. Ibid.

8. Ibid., 26.

9. Carolyn Mahaney, Nicole Mahaney Whitacre, Kristin Chesemore, and Janelle Bradshaw, *Shopping for Time* (Wheaton: Crossway, 2007), 85.

10. Hummel, *Tyranny of the Urgent*, 11.

11. Ibid., 17.

12. Ibid., 22.

13. Ibid., 26.

14. Ibid., 30.

**Part 3: The Reconnection**

1. *Merriam Webster Collegiate Dictionary*, 11th ed., s.v. "re."

**Chapter 12: The Reconnection**

1. Elisabeth Elliot, *A Lamp for My Feet* (Ann Arbor: Servant Publications, 1985), 56.

2. Cheryl Forbes, *Women of Devotion through the Centuries* (Grand Rapids:

Baker, 2001), 20. Note: Mrs. Cowman's books were published at a time when Americans were heavily influenced by the Scopes Monkey Trial and the writings of H. L. Mencken.

3. Elisabeth Elliot, *A Chance to Die* (Grand Rapids: Revell, 1987), 32.

4. Lawrence Kimbrough, *Words to Die For* (Nashville: B&H, 2002), 74.

5. Spiros Zodhiates, ed., *Hebrew-Greek Key Word Study Bible* (Chattanooga: AMG, 1990), 1821.

6. Charles W. Colson, *Loving God* (Grand Rapids: Zondervan, 1983), 213.

7. Ibid.

8. Ibid., 216.

9. John Piper, *Brothers, We Are Not Professionals* (Nashville: B&H, 2002), 79.

10. The Christian Arsenal, "Past Quotes of the Week," http://www.christian arsenal.com.

11. Chambers, *My Utmost for His Highest*, March 5.

12. Philip Yancey, *Disappointment with God* (Grand Rapids: Zondervan, 1988), 9.

13. Henri Nouwen, *Making All Things New* (New York: HarperCollins, 1981), 24.

14. Ibid.

15. Chambers, *My Utmost for His Highest*, March 5.

16. Jerry Sittser, *The Will of God as a Way of Life* (Grand Rapids: Zondervan, 2004), 183.

17. Chambers, *My Utmost for His Highest*, August 7.

18. Sittser, *The Will of God as a Way of Life*, 161.

# BECOME A LIFE-LONG PARTNER WITH GUIDESTONE FINANCIAL RESOURCES

As the wife of a pastor, you play an important part in working alongside your husband in his daily ministry and also in planning for your future. Although you and your husband will never "retire" from ministry, there will come a day when you will retire from vocational church service.

It is important to get started early in retirement planning. There is a thing called compound interest that is extremely powerful. For example, assuming an 8% annual return, if a twenty-five year old minister put fifty dollars per month in his retirement account it would be worth $174,550 at age sixty-five. If the same person waited until just the age of thirty-five to begin saving for retirement with the same fifty dollars per month it would be worth $74,520 at age sixty-five, a difference of $100,000. It is very important to start early, but it is also important to start wherever you are along the way to retirement.

Participants in eligible Southern Baptist churches receive an added benefit, the Protection Section, by being in GuideStone's Church Retirement Plan. If your husband, or your Southern Baptist church, contributes only a few dollars per month to the Church Retirement Plan, he will automatically receive at no cost to you or your church a survivor's benefit worth up to $100,000. He will also receive at no cost a $500 per month disability benefit simply by being a part of the Church Retirement Plan. This benefit is a cooperative effort provided by your state Baptist convention and GuideStone and is a safety net every Southern Baptist church should utilize for their ministers.

We at GuideStone want to be a life-long partner with your husband, and with you, throughout your entire ministry. This is the driving reason behind products that give you additional opportunities to save for retirement, or whatever your saving needs might be. You have available to you savings vehicles in addition to your regular 403(b) plan that include Personal Investing Accounts and IRAs (Traditional and Roth IRAs). These opportunities are also available to you as a spouse of a pastor eligible to participate in GuideStone plans.

**GuideStone**®
Financial Resources

For more information about these personal investing products, housing allowance advantages in retirement, or any of our other services,
visit us at www.GuideStone.org
or call us at 1-888-98GUIDE
and speak personally to one of our customer relations specialists.